P9-BAV-282

Glasgow

GREAT BRITAIN

Bristol

FRANCE

PORTUGAL

SPAIN

Lisbon

Cádiz

Gibraltar

Tangier

PIRATE WATERS

MOROCCO

Algiers

Tunis

TUNIS

Tripoli

ALGIERS

Benghazi

Derne

Alexandria

TRIPOLI

EGYPT

Malta

Mediterranean Sea

Constantinople

Black Sea

James Fort

Sierra Leone

THOMAS JEFFERSON

AND THE

TRIPOLI PIRATES

ALSO BY BRIAN KILMEADE AND DON YAEGER

George Washington's Secret Six

BRIAN KILMEADE

AND DON YAEGER

THOMAS JEFFERSON

★ ★ ★ ★ ★ AND THE ★ ★ ★ ★ ★

TRIPOLI PIRATES

THE FORGOTTEN WAR THAT CHANGED AMERICAN HISTORY

SENTINEL

SENTINEL
An imprint of Penguin Random House LLC
375 Hudson Street
New York, New York 10014
penguin.com

Photo insert page 3 (top left): Stephen Decatur (1779–1820), by Rembrandt Peale, ca. 1815–1820; oil on canvas; overall: 29 x 23 5/8 in (73.7 x 60 cm); 1867.309, New-York Historical Society

Photo insert page 5 (bottom left): The attack made on Tripoli on the 3rd August 1804…; from PR100 (Maritime File), FF 56—Barbary War; neg #3516, New-York Historical Society

Photo insert page 6 (middle): Blowing up the fire ship *Intrepid*; from PR100 (Maritime File), FF 56, FF E, Drawer; Med Naval Battles: Barbary War; neg #90696d, New-York Historical Society

Photo insert page 7 (middle): General William Eaton and Hamet Qaramanli, *On the Desert of Barca, Approaching Derne*; from "Memories of a Hundred Years," p. 60, E173, H16 v. 1; neg #90916d, New-York Historical Society

Photo insert page 8 (bottom): The U.S. Squadron, under Command of Com. Decatur, At Anchor off the City of Algiers, June 30, 1815; from PR100 (Maritime File), box 11, folder 8; neg #90695d, New-York Historical Society

Additional credits appear adjacent to the respective images.

ISBN_978-1-59184-806-6

Printed in the United States of America
10 9 8 7 6 5 4 3 2 1

Set in Bulmer MT Std
Design and Map Illustrations by Daniel Lagin

*To my dad, who died way too young, and my mom,
who worked way too hard. They taught me from day one
that being born in America was like winning the lottery.
This story is yet more proof that they were 100 percent right.*

—BK

*To Jeanette: I adore you. Thanks for encouraging this
relationship, making this book happen.*

—DY

CONTENTS

CONTENTS

CONTENTS

CAST OF CHARACTERS

Sidi Haji Abdrahaman: Tripolitan Envoy to Great Britain

John Adams: Minister to the Court of St. James's, later President of the United States

William Bainbridge: Captain, U.S. Navy

Joel Barlow: Consul General to the Barbary States

Samuel Barron: Captain, U.S. Navy, commander of the USS *President*

Salvador Catalano: Pilot, USS *Intrepid*

James Leander Cathcart: U.S. Consul to Tripoli

Richard Dale: Captain, U.S. Navy

James Decatur: Lieutenant, U.S. Navy, Gunboat No. 2

Stephen Decatur Jr.: Lieutenant, U.S. Navy

William Eaton: U.S. Consul General to Tunis

Daniel Frazier: Ordinary Seaman, U.S. Navy, Gunboat No. 5

Albert Gallatin: Secretary of the Treasury

Hassan: Dey of Algiers*

Isaac Hull: Captain, U.S. Navy, USS *Argus*

Martha and Mary (Polly) Jefferson: Daughters of Thomas Jefferson

Thomas Jefferson: Minister to France, later President of the United States

Ahmed Khorshid: Viceroy of Egypt

Tobias Lear: U.S. Consul General to the Barbary States

James Madison: Secretary of State, later President of the United States

Richard Valentine Morris: Captain, U.S. Navy, commander of the USS *Chesapeake*

Alexander Murray: Captain, U.S. Navy, commander of the USS *Constellation*

Bobba Mustapha: Dey of Algiers

Nicholas Nissen: Danish Consul General

Presley Neville O'Bannon: Lieutenant, U.S. Marines

Richard O'Brien: Captain of the *Dauphin*

---

* Though sometimes used interchangeably in diplomatic correspondence ca. 1800, the titles *Dey*, *Bey*, and *Bashaw* (sometimes rendered *Pasha*) will in the pages that follow distinguish the regency rulers dey of Algiers, bey of Tunis, and bashaw of Tripoli.

CAST OF CHARACTERS

Edward Preble: Captain, U.S. Navy, commander of the USS *Constitution*

Hamet Qaramanli: Brother of Yusuf and rightful heir as Bashaw of Tripoli

Yusuf Qaramanli: Bashaw of Tripoli

Murat Rais: High Admiral, Navy of Tripoli (formerly Peter Lisle)

Mahomet Rous: Admiral, Navy of Tripoli, commander of the *Tripoli*

Richard Somers: Master Commandant, U.S. Navy, USS *Intrepid*

Andrew Sterett: Lieutenant, U.S. Navy, commander of the USS *Enterprise*

Maulay Sulaiman: Sultan of Morocco

George Washington: President of the United States

AUTHOR'S NOTE

I t is my observation that American history has been for the most part focused on the genius of our founding fathers and not enough on those who fought and died for their ideals. We have written *Thomas Jefferson and the Tripoli Pirates* for those men and women who have been forgotten by most, though they were saluted in their day.

This is the story of how a new nation, saddled with war debt and desperate to establish credibility, was challenged by four Muslim powers. Our merchant ships were captured and the crews enslaved. Despite its youth, America would do what established western powers chose not to do: stand up to intimidation and lawlessness.

Tired of Americans being captured and held for ransom, our third president decided to take on the Barbary powers in a war that is barely remembered today but is one that, in many ways, we are still fighting.

In the following pages you will read how Jefferson, the so-called pacifist president, changed George Washington's and John Adams's policies to take on this collection of Muslim nations. You will travel alongside the fearless William Eaton as he treks five hundred miles

across the desert. You will learn about the leadership of Stephen Decatur and Edward Preble, and about the fighting prowess of Marine
lieutenant Presley O'Bannon, just to name a few. You will discover
how the Marine Corps emerged as the essential military force it is
today. Most important, you will see the challenges Presidents Washington, Adams, Jefferson, and Madison faced with the Barbary nations. And you will learn how military strength and the courage of
our first generation of Americans led to victory, and ultimately respect in a world of nations that believed—and even hoped—that the
American experiment would fail. Because of these brave men, the
world would learn that in America failure is not an option.

I love this story and the brave men who secured our freedom. If
this book does anything to restore them to America's memory, it will
have succeeded.

—Brian Kilmeade

THOMAS JEFFERSON
AND THE
TRIPOLI PIRATES

PROLOGUE

Unprepared and Unprotected

Picture to yourself your Brother Citizens or Unfortunate
Countrymen in the Algerian State Prisons or Damned Cas-
tile, and starved 2/3rd's and Naked. . . . Once a Citizen of the
United States of America, but at present the Most Miserable
Slave in Algiers.

—**Richard O'Brien**, *Diary*, **February 19, 1790**

s a fast-moving ship approached the *Dauphin* off the coast
of Portugal, Captain Richard O'Brien saw no cause for
alarm. On this warm July day in 1785, America was at
peace, and there were many innocent reasons for a friendly ship to
come alongside. Perhaps it was a fellow merchant ship needing information or supplies. Perhaps the ship's captain wanted to warn him of
nearby pirates.

By the time O'Brien realized that the ship did not approach in
peace, it was too late. The American ship was no match for the Algerian vessel armed with fourteen cannons. A raiding party with daggers gripped between their teeth swarmed over the sides of the

1

Dauphin. The Algerians vastly outnumbered the American crew and quickly claimed the ship and all its goods in the name of their nation's leader, the dey of Algiers.

Mercilessly, the pirates stripped O'Brien and his men of shoes, hats, and handkerchiefs, leaving them unprotected from the burning sun during the twelve-day voyage back to the North African coast. On arrival in Algiers, the American captives were paraded through the streets as spectators jeered.

The seamen were issued rough sets of native clothing and two blankets each that were to last for the entire period of captivity, whether it was a few weeks or fifty years. Kept in a slave pen, they slept on a stone floor, gazing into the night sky where the hot stars burned above them like lidless eyes, never blinking. Each night there was a roll call, and any man who failed to respond promptly would be chained to a column and whipped soundly in the morning.

Together with men of another captured ship, the *Maria*, O'Brien's *Dauphin* crew broke rocks in the mountains while wearing iron chains Saturday through Thursday. On Friday, the Muslim holy day, the Christian slaves dragged massive sleds loaded with rubble and dirt nearly two miles to the harbor to be unloaded into the sea to form a breakwater. Their workdays began before the sun rose and, for a few blissfully cool hours, they worked in darkness.

Their diet consisted of stale bread, vinegar from a shared bowl at breakfast and lunch, and, on good days, some ground olives. Water was the one necessity provided with any liberality. As a ship captain, O'Brien was treated somewhat better, but he feared that his men would starve to death.

"Our sufferings are beyond our expression or your conception," O'Brien wrote to America's minister to France, Thomas Jefferson, two weeks after his arrival in Algiers.[1] Those sufferings would only get worse. Several of the captives from the *Maria* and the *Dauphin* would die in captivity of yellow fever, overwork, and exposure—and in some ways, they were the lucky ones. The ways out of prison for the remaining prisoners were few: convert to Islam, attempt to escape, or wait for their country to negotiate their release. A few of the captives would be ransomed but, for most, their thin blankets wore out as year after year passed and freedom remained out of reach. Richard O'Brien would be ten years a slave.

America had not yet elected its first president, but it already had its first enemy.

CHAPTER 1

Americans Abroad

It is not probable the American States will have a very free trade in the Mediterranean . . . the Americans cannot protect themselves [as] they cannot pretend to [have] a Navy.

—John Baker-Holroyd, Lord Sheffield, *Observations of the Commerce of the American States,* 1783

In 1785, the same year Richard O'Brien was captured by pirates, Thomas Jefferson learned that all politics, even transatlantic politics, are personal.

He was a widower. The passing of his wife in September 1782 had left him almost beyond consolation, and what little comfort he found was in the company of his daughter Martha, then age ten. The two would take "melancholy rambles" around the large plantation, seeking to evade the grief that haunted them. When Jefferson was offered the appointment as American minister to France, he accepted because he saw an opportunity to escape the sadness that still shadowed him.

Thomas Jefferson had sailed for Europe in the summer of 1784 with Martha at his side; once they reached Paris, he enrolled his daughter in a convent school with many other well-born English-speaking students. There he would be able to see her regularly, but he had been forced to make a more difficult decision regarding Martha's two sisters. Mary, not yet six, and toddler Lucy Elizabeth, both too young to travel with him across the sea, had been left behind with their "Aunt Eppes," his late wife's half sister. The separation was painful, but it was nothing compared with the new heartbreak he experienced just months into his Paris stay when Mrs. Eppes wrote sadly to say that "hooping cough" had taken the life of two-year-old Lucy.[1]

As a fresh wave of sorrow rolled over him, Jefferson longed for "Polly the Parrot," as he affectionately called his bright and talkative Mary, to join his household again. The father wrote to his little girl that he and her sister "cannot live without you" and asked her if she would like to join them across the ocean. He promised that joining them in France meant she would learn "to play on the harpsichord, to draw, to dance, to read and talk French."[2]

"I long to see you, and hope that you . . . are well," the now seven-year-old replied. But she added that she had no desire to make the trip, harpsichord or no harpsichord. "I don't want to go to France," she stated plainly. "I had rather stay with Aunt Eppes."[3]

Jefferson was undaunted and began to plan for her safe travel. Having already lost two dear family members, he did not want to risk losing Polly and looked for ways to reduce the dangers of the journey. He instructed her uncle, Francis Eppes, to select a proven ship for Polly's crossing. "The vessel should have performed one [transatlantic] voyage at least," Jefferson ordered, "and must not be more than four or five years old."[4] He worried about the weather and insisted that his daughter travel in the warm months to avoid winter storms. As for supervision, Polly could make the journey, Jefferson advised, "with some good lady passing from America to France, or even England [or] . . . a careful gentleman."[5]

Yet an even more intimidating concern worried Jefferson: more frightening than weather or leaky ships was the threat of pirates off North Africa, a region known as the Barbary Coast. The fate of the *Dauphin* and the *Maria* was a common one for ships venturing near the area, where the Sahara's arid coast was divided into four nation-states. Running west to east were the Barbary nations Morocco, Algiers, Tunis, and Tripoli, which all fell under the ultimate authority of the Ottoman Empire, seated in present-day Turkey.

The Islamic nations of the Barbary Coast had preyed upon foreign shipping for centuries, attacking ships in international waters

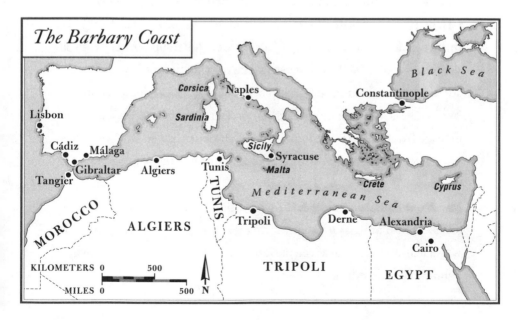

The Barbary Coast

both in the Mediterranean and along the northwest coast of Africa and the Iberian peninsula. Even such naval powers as France and Great Britain were not immune, though they chose to deal with the problem by paying annual tributes of "gifts" to Barbary leaders— bribes paid to the Barbary states to persuade the pirates to leave merchant ships from the paying countries alone. But the prices were always changing, and the ships of those nations that did not meet the extortionate demands were not safe from greedy pirates.

To the deeply rational Jefferson, the lawless pirates posed perhaps the greatest danger to his sadly diminished family. He knew what had happened to O'Brien and could not risk a similar fate for his child. As he confided in a letter to brother-in-law Francis Eppes, "My anxieties on this subject could induce me to endless details. . . . The Algerines this fall took two vessels from us and now have twenty-two of our citizens in slavery." The plight of the men aboard the *Maria* and the *Dauphin* haunted him—if their hellish incarceration was terrifying to contemplate, "who can estimate . . . the fate of a child? My mind revolts at the possibility of a capture," Jefferson wrote. "Unless you hear from myself—not trusting the information of any other person on earth—that peace is made with the Algerines, do not send her but in a vessel of French or English property; for these vessels alone are safe from prize by the barbarians."[6] He knew those two countries paid a very high annual tribute, thereby purchasing safe passage for their vessels.

As a father, he could feel in his bones a fear for his daughter's safety. As an ambassador and an American, Jefferson recognized it was a fear no citizen of a free nation embarking on an oceanic voyage should have to endure.

A MEETING OF MINISTERS

A few months later, in March 1786, Jefferson would make his way to London to meet with his good friend John Adams. Together they hoped to figure out how to deal with the emerging threat to American interests.

His waistline thickening, his chin growing jowly, fifty-year-old John Adams welcomed Jefferson into his London home. Overlooking the tree-lined Grosvenor Square from the town house Adams had rented, the two men sat down to talk in the spacious drawing room.

Adams was the United States' first ambassador to Great Britain. Just arrived from Paris after a cold and blustery six-day journey, Jefferson was minister to the French government of Louis XVI. To Adams and his wife, Abigail, their old friend looked different, as Jefferson had begun powdering his ginger hair white. The stout New Englander and the tall, lean, forty-two-year-old Virginian might have been of different breeds—but then, in the years to come, they would often be of two minds in their political thinking as well.

Unlike most of the European diplomats they encountered, neither Adams nor Jefferson had been born into a tradition of diplomatic decorum. Adams was a rough-and-tumble lawyer, the son of a yeoman farmer from south of Boston, known for a damn-all attitude of speaking his mind. A man of quiet natural grace, Jefferson was learning the cosmopolitan ways of Paris but, at heart, he was a well-born country boy, heir to large farms outside Charlottesville, a tiny courthouse town in central Virginia. Both men were novices in the game of international negotiation, a game their country needed them to learn quickly.

When the Americans and British signed the Treaty of Paris in 1783, bringing to an end the Revolution, the United States' legal status changed in the view of every nation and world leader. No longer under British protection, the fledgling nation found that its status was lowly indeed. Adams's letters to the British government tended to go unanswered, and Jefferson's attempts to negotiate trade treaties with France and Spain were going nowhere. Now a more hostile international threat was rearing its head, and Adams had summoned Jefferson from Paris to discuss the danger posed by the "piratical nations" of North Africa.

In earlier days, the colonies' ships had enjoyed the protection offered by the Union Jack; but because U.S. ships no longer carried British passports, the British navy provided no protection against pirates. The French, America's wartime allies against the British, did not protect them now that there was peace. Americans abroad were very much on their own, especially in international waters. And because America had no navy to protect its interests, insurance for American ships skyrocketed to twenty times the rate of that of European ships.[7]

The expense of insurance was insupportable, but America's economy could not afford to end trade on the high seas; the Revolution had been fought with borrowed money, and repayment of those debts depended upon ongoing international commerce. One key piece of the nation's economic health was trade with southern Europe, accessible only by sailing into the Mediterranean—and within range of the Barbary pirates. According to Jefferson's calculations, a quarter of New England's most important export, dried salt cod, went to markets there, as did one sixth of the country's grain exports. Rice and lumber were also important exports, and the merchant ships provided employment for more than a thousand seamen. The trade and employment were essential to the growing American economy, and John Adams thought the numbers could easily double if a diplomatic solution in the Barbary region could be reached.

The American government had initially approved payment to the North African nations. But the bribes demanded were impossibly high, many hundreds of thousands of dollars when the American treasury could afford only token offerings of a few tens of thousands. In an era when not a single American was worth a million dollars, and Mr. Jefferson's great house, Monticello, was assessed at seventy-five hundred dollars, paying such exorbitant bribes seemed almost incomprehensible. Unable to pay enough to buy the goodwill of the Barbary countries, America was forced to let its ships sail at their own risk. Sailors like those on the *Maria* and the *Dauphin* had become pawns in a very dangerous game.

On this day, Adams and Jefferson worried over the fate of the *Dauphin* and the *Maria*. It had been nearly a year since the pirates from Algiers had taken the ships and cargoes the previous July, and now the regent of Algiers had made known his demand: until he was paid an exorbitant and, it seemed, ever-escalating ransom, the American captives were to be his slaves.

Despite their pity for the captives, Jefferson and Adams knew the new nation couldn't afford a new war or a new source of debt. They understood that the cost of keeping American ships away from the Barbary Coast would be greater than the cost of addressing the problem. That left the two American ministers, as Jefferson confided to a friend, feeling "absolutely suspended between indignation and impotence."[8]

Yet neither Jefferson nor Adams could afford to remain paralyzed in the face of the danger. Not only had American families and the economy been endangered, but rumor had it that the pirates had also captured a ship carrying the venerable Benjamin Franklin, Jefferson's predecessor as minister to France. (As one of his correspondents wrote to Franklin, "We are waiting with the greatest patience to hear from you. The newspapers have given us anxiety on your account; for some of them insist that you have been taken by the Algerines, while others pretend that you are at Morocco, enduring your slavery with all the patience of a philosopher."[9]) To everyone's relief, the reports proved false, but the scare brought the very real dangers posed by the Barbary pirates too close for comfort.

Sitting in the London house, John Adams and Thomas Jefferson discussed the idea of a negotiation that might break the impasse. Adams had a new reason to hope that the Barbary rulers could be reasoned with, and the two ministers set about deciding upon the right approach.

"MONEY IS THEIR GOD AND MAHOMET THEIR PROPHET"

A few weeks earlier, Adams had made an unannounced visit to the Barbary state of Tripoli's ambassador, freshly arrived in London. To Adams's surprise, the bearded Sidi Haji Abdrahaman had welcomed him warmly. Seated in front of a roaring fire, with two servants in attendance, they smoked tobacco from great pipes with six-foot-long stems "fit for a Walking Cane." Adams had promptly written to Jefferson. "It is long since I took a pipe, but [we] smoked in awful pomp, reciprocating whiff for whiff . . . until coffee was brought in."[10]

Adams made a strong impression on the Tripolitans. Observing his expertise with the Turkish smoking device, an attendant praised his technique, saying, *"Monsieur, vous êtes un Turk!"* ("Sir, you are a Turk!")[11] It was a high compliment.

Abdrahaman returned Adams's visit two days later, and Adams decided his new diplomatic acquaintance was "a benevolent and wise man" with whom the United States could do business.[12] He believed Abdrahaman might help broker an arrangement between the United States and the other Barbary nations, bringing an end to the capture of American merchantmen. Now reunited with his friend and fellow American, he shared his plan with Jefferson and invited him to join the conversation.

On a blustery March day, Adams, Jefferson, and Abdrahaman convened at the house of the Tripolitan envoy. The conversation began in an improvised mix of broken French and Italian, as the Tripolitan envoy spoke little English. The discussion was cordial, and Adams and Jefferson began to believe that a solution was in sight. When the talk turned to money, however, the bubble of optimism soon exploded.

Jefferson had researched the sums paid as tribute by European countries, including Denmark, Sweden, and Portugal, so he knew the going rate. But the gold Abdrahaman demanded that day was beyond the reach of the United States: a perpetual peace with Tripoli would cost some 30,000 English guineas, the equivalent of roughly $120,000, not counting the 10 percent gratuity Abdrahaman demanded for himself. And that amount bought peace with only one of the Barbary states. To buy peace in Tunis would cost another 30,000 guineas, to say nothing of what would be required to pay Morocco or even Algiers, the largest and most powerful of the four.

The $80,000 that Congress had been hard-pressed to authorize for an across-the-board understanding was no more than a down payment on what would be needed to meet the Barbary demands.[13]

Although he now despaired of an easy solution, Adams wasn't ready to stop talking. He could understand financial concerns, and he was already beginning to realize what O'Brien would later say of the pirates: "Money is their God and Mahomet their Prophet."[14] Yet greed alone couldn't explain the madness and cruelty of the demands. Unsatisfied, the famously blunt Adams wanted a better answer. While maintaining the best diplomatic reserve he could muster—whatever their frustration, the American ministers could hardly leap to their feet and walk out of the negotiations—Adams asked how the Barbary states could justify "[making] war upon nations who had done them no injury."

The response was nothing less than chilling.

According to his holy book, the Qur'an, Abdrahaman explained, "all nations which had not acknowledged the Prophet were sinners, whom it was the right and duty of the faithful to plunder and enslave."

Christian sailors were, plain and simple, fair game.

Jefferson tried to make sense of what he was hearing. He was familiar with the Muslim holy book. He had purchased a copy of the Qur'an during his days of reading law in Williamsburg twenty years before but found its values so foreign that he shelved the volume with books devoted to the mythology of the Greeks and Romans. This conversation left him even more perplexed. The man who had written that all people were "endowed by their Creator with certain inalienable rights" was horrified at Abdrahaman's religious justification for greed and cruelty.

Dashing Adams's high hopes, Abdrahaman refused to play the role of "benevolent and wise man." Despite the Americans' horror, he wasn't apologizing in any way. He showed no remorse or regret. He believed the actions of his fellow Muslims fully justified.

"Every mussulman," he explained, "who was slain in this warfare was sure to go to paradise."

To Abdrahaman, this was not complicated. In his culture, the takers of ships, the enslavers of men, the Barbarians who extorted bribes for safe passage, were all justified by the teaching of the prophet Muhammad. "It was written in our Qur'an," he said simply.[15]

When the meeting ended, the two American ministers, disheartened and outraged, left empty-handed. They had found no solution, no peaceful answer to protecting American shipping or freeing their countrymen enslaved in North Africa.

THE PRICE OF PEACE

Their initial attempt at making peace foiled, Adams and Jefferson began to plan their next approach. They agreed that the status quo was not workable, but that's where their agreement ended.

In the coming months, the two old friends would find they disagreed about how to deal with the Barbary pirates. Adams remained determined to continue the negotiations. The Americans should be willing to pay for peace, he believed, even if they had to borrow money to pay the tributes. "If it is not done," he wrote to Jefferson from London that summer, "you and I . . . ought to go home."[16]

In Paris, Jefferson expressed another view. He did not wish to "buy a peace," as he put it. He did not trust the Barbary powers to keep their word. At the same time, he did not think America could afford to stop trading with the Mediterranean. He believed in freedom on the seas, and he proposed a tougher position.

"I should prefer the obtaining of it by war," he wrote to Adams from France.[17] Jefferson argued that America needed a navy to deal with the pirates of the Barbary coast, to confront and destroy them.

He told Adams that justice, honor, and the respect of Europe for the United States would be served by establishing a fleet in "constant cruise" in Barbary waters, policing and confronting ships of the outlaw states as necessary. He argued that an armed naval presence made budgetary sense. According to his calculations, establishing a small navy would be less costly than the sum of the ransoms, bribes, and maritime losses.

Adams disagreed. He believed that a war against the Islamic nations would be costly and possibly unwinnable. It would certainly require too large a military force for America's budget. Opposing Jefferson's belief that a small navy could solve the problem, he told Jefferson, "We ought not to fight them at all unless We determine to fight them forever."[18]

Despite their differences, the two men worked tirelessly to gain the freedom of the enslaved sailors. They sent American agents to conduct negotiations with the Barbary governments. Jefferson contacted the Mathurins, also called Trinitarians, a Catholic religious order that had worked to free Christian captives since 1199. All efforts failed. O'Brien and his men remained in captivity, and eventually diplomacy between the United States and Algiers went quiet. More than five years would pass before American negotiators would return to Algiers to resume talks. During those years, several hundred more Christian men, women, and children would join the ranks of the imprisoned, as the pirates collected more ships, booty, and slaves.

But the situation continued to trouble Jefferson deeply. Remembering his fear for Polly's safety, he sympathized with the terrible worry and sleepless nights that American families endured on behalf of loved ones who made a living on the sea. In a world where the Barbary pirates roamed the eastern Atlantic and the Mediterranean, who would they capture and enslave next? Would the next captives ever make it home again, or would they die of disease or under the lash in a foreign land?

The Barbary powers, with their mixture of greed, religious fanaticism, and self-interest, would not listen to reason. They might listen to force, but with no navy, the Americans could not bring power to bear on the pirates. Both Adams and Jefferson were stymied and returned to America without solutions, but they did not give up entirely. Soon enough, Jefferson would confront the issue from a fresh vantage.

CHAPTER 2

Secretary Jefferson

It rests with Congress to decide between war, tribute, and ransom, as the means of re-establishing our Mediterranean commerce.

—Secretary of State Thomas Jefferson, December 30, 1790

W hen Thomas Jefferson stepped ashore in Norfolk, Virginia, in November 1789, he was shocked when the mayor and aldermen of the town greeted him with words of congratulation on his new appointment as George Washington's secretary of state.

During Jefferson's five years abroad, the political landscape in the United States had changed. The U.S. Constitution had been drafted and ratified, and General George Washington had taken office as the first president on April 30, 1789. Though Jefferson had still been in Europe, the president had chosen him to serve in the newly created post of secretary of state and Congress had confirmed the appointment during Jefferson's crossing.

As he absorbed the news, Jefferson was both humbled and honored that George Washington had appointed him for the daunting task. Except for matters of finance and war, the secretary of state would administer the entire government. Jefferson asked for time to consider, but back at home that winter in central Virginia, he decided to accept the appointment. He remained at his mountaintop home, Monticello, to witness the February marriage of daughter Martha, now seventeen, then he traveled to New York, temporarily the nation's capital, to join the government.

At their very first meeting, on March 22, 1790, the president and his new secretary of state discussed an issue that had been weighing on Jefferson for years—the plight of Richard O'Brien and his men.

Washington and Jefferson weren't the only Americans worrying about their captive countrymen. On May 14, 1790, a petition was read on the floor of Congress. The captured men had sent a letter to Congress asking it to intervene on their behalf as their situation grew more desperate and the outlook even bleaker as the years passed.

Congress's interest in the problem went beyond the enslaved men, because the continuing threat to ships had meant that American trade in the Mediterranean was dwindling—at a great cost to the otherwise healthy American economy. Congress and the president wasted no time, immediately referring the matter to the new secretary of state; with Washington's mandate, Jefferson set about examining the issue in detail.

A bookish man by nature, Jefferson began by looking into the history of the Barbary pirates. He planned to spend months researching the pirates' centuries-long practice of enslaving innocent sailors before making definitive suggestions for action. As he compiled an exhaustive report on the problem, he also corresponded with Richard O'Brien, who remained a prisoner of the Algerians.

Because O'Brien had the rank of sea captain, his experience in captivity was far better than that of most other prisoners, and he had been assigned relatively comfortable work at the British consulate, tilling soil, planting trees, and feeding the pigs before eventually rising to become a liaison to the dey. That privileged position allowed him to travel to Portugal, England, and Germany to beg for ransom gold from governments, private parties, and Christian aid groups. He was heavily guarded on such journeys, unable to make his escape; he also knew that if he did not return, things would be much worse for the men he left behind—men who were already subjected to hard labor and harsh treatment.

O'Brien did what he could to answer the questions Jefferson posed to him in his letters, and on December 30, 1790, President Washington laid before both houses of Congress the results of Jefferson's meticulous research. There were two reports, titled "Prisoners at Algiers" and "Mediterranean Trade."

Although his papers seemed to support the ransom strategy, Jefferson had his doubts. He maintained his long-standing skepticism about a purchased peace. For years, even before the capture of the *Dauphin* and the *Maria* and his subsequent disagreement with Adams, Jefferson had called for America to use the navy to solve the problem of the Barbary pirates. Seven years before, he had written of his objections to paying tribute. If negotiations broke down (as indeed they had, repeatedly, in the years since), what then?

If they refuse a [fair treaty], why not go to war with them? We ought to begin a naval power if we mean to carry on our own commerce. Can we begin it on a more honorable occasion, or with a weaker foe? I am of opinion [that] with half a dozen frigates [we could] totally destroy their commerce.[1]

In his 1790 reports to Congress, the ever-thorough Jefferson presented detailed intelligence he had collected on the size of the naval force at Algiers and its tactics. He wasn't impressed with the Algerians' poorly equipped ships, pointing out that their battle strategies depended on boarding their target ships, rather than on their cannons.[2] He hinted that the Americans would need only a small navy to beat the pirates, but, perhaps caving to political pressure, he stopped short of calling for direct military action. "It rests with Congress to decide between war, tribute, and ransom," he concluded, "as the means of re-establishing our Mediterranean commerce."[3]

Some senators considered instituting a navy, but the nation's empty treasury ended the conversation about warships even before it got started. Ransom seemed cheaper, but the process for funding it was excruciatingly slow; it wasn't until more than a year later, in 1792, that the sum of $40,000 was authorized for a treaty with Algiers. Then distance and death increased the delay—the two men appointed to negotiate with Algiers both died of natural causes before talks could begin—so it wasn't until 1794 that any negotiations started.

O'Brien and his men, enslaved for nine years, still waited for freedom.

BUILDING A NAVY

When Jefferson became secretary of state, his nation had no navy. The last of the ships in the Continental Navy, made legendary by John Paul Jones, had been sold off after the Revolution. There had been no money to maintain them, and no threat close enough to home to justify raising funds.

The dismantling of the navy had suited President Washington perfectly. Over and over again he said he favored a policy of strict neutrality in international affairs, a position he made explicit in his "Neutrality Proclamation" of 1793. Recalling the terrible toll of the Revolution on the nation's people and resources, Washington wished to fight no more wars. He desired neither a standing army nor a navy.

That Washington and Jefferson did not see eye-to-eye on many issues was one of the worst-kept secrets in Washington. Jefferson took issue with what he perceived to be Washington's poor judgment of character, as he mentioned in an ill-advised letter that ended up being published widely. Based on his earlier years in Europe, Jefferson also believed sound judgment of the Barbary situation called for military action. He would submit to his president but push where he could.

His influence seems to have worked. A matter of months after Jefferson joined the cabinet, the political tide turned. In October 1793, the secretary of state received a desperate letter from the U.S. consul in Lisbon. A new attack fleet of Algerian ships roamed the Atlantic near Gibraltar. The flotilla consisted of eight ships, including four frigates and a twenty-gun brig. Their objective? "To cruise against the American flag."[4] The growing wealth of the United States had caught the pirates' attention. No longer would they attack just the

American vessels unlucky enough to cross their paths, but they were now actively seeking out American ships. "I have not slept since Receipt of the news of this hellish plot," the consul wrote Jefferson. "Another corsair in the Atlantic—God preserve us—."[5]

Soon a new dispatch from Gibraltar reported that ten American vessels had been captured in late October. Not only had the Algerians taken more ships, but they had also added 110 captives to their slave pens. The pirate problem could be ignored no longer, nor simply be debated. Action was required.

In Congress, a House committee was appointed to study the sort of ships needed. It soon reported back, and House debate, beginning on February 16, 1794, lasted a month. Jefferson's own Republican party, led by his dear friend and confidant Congressman James Madison, took a stance different from Jefferson's, believing that a navy would unnecessarily expand the federal government. The Federalists, using Jefferson's old argument, reasoned that the cost of establishing a navy would be less than the cost of *not* having one. Maritime insurance rates continued to skyrocket, and the cost of imported goods grew by the day. A navy, they argued, had become economically necessary.

Despite the bitter division between parties and regions—New England delegations tended to want a navy to protect their merchants while Southerners generally opposed such federal expansion—the House reached a compromise, agreeing to halt ship construction if peace was achieved. Both houses of Congress passed the Act to Provide a Naval Armament by narrow margins. Signed into law by President Washington on March 27, 1794, the act authorized the purchase or construction of six frigates, four rated for forty-four guns, two for thirty-six guns. The immense sum of $688,888 was appropriated.

Thus it had been decided: the United States would have a navy. George Washington ordered the shipbuilding contracts spread out between northern and southern ports, and construction began. Three years would pass before the first frigate was launched, and during that time, the chess match that was Barbary diplomacy would see the rules of the game shift again and again. With every failed negotiation, it would become increasingly clear that only one solution remained: those frigates would have to cross the ocean and try a different kind of diplomacy, one that came from the mouths of their canons.

BLEEDING US DRY

As 1793 ended, Jefferson resigned, retiring to Monticello to consider his future. In the year after his departure, the United States managed to reach a peace agreement with the dey of Algiers—a deal that meant that, against Jefferson's advice, Americans would pay for peace. Though there was no longer any immediate need for more naval ships, President Washington did persuade Congress that stopping the shipbuilding would be unwise.

Washington's instincts proved sound. Because the Americans were perennially slow in making their transatlantic payments of tribute, the dey threatened war and refused to release the prisoners. The Americans were relieved that they had kept the shipbuilding going, and the USS *United States*, USS *Constellation*, and USS *Constitution* launched in 1797.

By 1797, Joel Barlow was on duty as ambassador to the volatile leader of Algiers. The president had dispatched him the previous year to "take charge of the interests of the United States of America within the Regency of Algiers."[6] His goal was to maintain the peace—and gain the release of O'Brien and his men.

If anyone was equipped for the difficult diplomacy needed in Algiers, Barlow was. A Yale graduate who had served in the Revolution, worked as a newspaperman, and been imprisoned during the French Revolution, he had emerged after the Reign of Terror as an honorary citizen of France. Barlow seemed like the man to deal with whatever came his way. He had the brains, the courage, and the courtly manner to be an expert diplomat—but it wasn't clear that that would be enough to rescue the American slaves.

When Barlow arrived as American consul to Algiers, he was confronted with the dey's refusal to release the prisoners until the United States fulfilled its monetary promises. Barlow gave his word that payment was forthcoming but, in the meantime, plied the Algerian ruler with diamond rings, brocade robes, carpets, jeweled snuffboxes, and other goods he had brought with him from France, treasures worth more than $27,000. Some mix of personality, placating gifts, and promises of money persuaded the dey, who—at last—released the prisoners. Their ranks had been reduced by harsh prison conditions and illness, but Barlow guided eighty-five survivors aboard the ship *Fortune*, and watched them depart for friendlier shores.

After O'Brien and the other captives went free, Barlow and his fellow American consuls in the region remained behind to finish a series of impossibly complicated negotiations. Committed to purchasing a treaty, he put up with diplomatic chicanery, delays, broken promises, and shaky deals. Bowing to the Algerians' humiliating demands, the American government would agree to hand over money and goods worth close to a million dollars, a cost equal to one eighth of the federal government's annual expenditures.

Because the United States didn't have the cash on hand to pay the dey, the money had to be borrowed. Richard O'Brien, who had chosen to remain behind after his shipmates were free in order to assist the American government, was by then a well-known and well-connected presence in Algiers from his years of working at the British consulate. Traveling to several cities in Europe, including London, hoping to obtain gold and silver from London bankers he finally succeeded in securing loans in Portugal and Italy, but, before the money reached Algiers, O'Brien's bad luck resurfaced. The ship he traveled on, the brig *Sophia,* was taken by Tripolitan pirates.

Because the ship had an Algerian passport, Bashaw Yusuf Qaramanli, ruler of Tripoli, promptly ordered its release. But O'Brien's capture gave Barlow an idea: he commissioned O'Brien to act as his intermediary and to negotiate with the militant bashaw.

Ruthless and cunning, Bashaw Yusuf had murdered one brother for the throne and exiled another brother, Hamet, the rightful bashaw, holding Hamet's family hostage to guarantee that he would not return to fight for his birthright. Whether the Americans would be able to successfully negotiate with such a man was unclear, but Barlow deemed it worth an attempt and the Treaty of Peace and Friendship Between the United States and Tripoli was signed in November 1796. It included the usual provisions, one for payment of tribute, another for the delivery of maritime and military stores, in return for free passage of American ships and mutual cooperation.

The treaty was ratified by the United States Congress in June 1797 and Barlow returned to France, having spent only two years in

North Africa, but leaving two new treaties in place. Two more—with the remaining Barbary states, Morocco and Tunis—would shortly be signed. Between the treaties and the freeing of the long-imprisoned sailors, Barlow's brief tenure had been a success.

Jefferson seemed to have been wrong about the necessity of force. For the moment, the United States of America and the Barbary Coast states enjoyed a purchased peace—but the Americans' new warships waited in the wings, just in case.

ENTER EATON

After Barlow's departure, a team of highly qualified men was commissioned to represent the United States in the Barbary region. At its head was Richard O'Brien, named in December 1797 to succeed Barlow as consul general to all the Barbary states.

In December 1798, another former captive, James Leander Cathcart, joined O'Brien in North Africa, assuming the post of American consul to Tripoli. Cathcart had been aboard the *Maria* when it was captured in 1785 and had also endured a decade of captivity alongside O'Brien. No stranger to harsh conditions, having spent time on a British prison ship during the Revolution prior to his Algerian enslavement, Cathcart had known how to promote himself when he found himself a prisoner once again. During his years in Algiers, he had risen slowly in the estimation of his captors, becoming a clerk and overseer before his appointment as secretary to the dey in 1792. From that post he had been able to hobnob with men of considerable power, including the Swedish consul, who eventually loaned him $5,000 to gain his freedom. But he wasn't a man who wore the hardships of his Algerian years easily.

Cathcart crossed the Atlantic in the company of the new American consul to Tunis, William Eaton, whose prematurely white hair and cleft chin gave him the appearance of a Roman general carved out of marble. A driven man of many talents, Eaton had been chosen by Secretary of State Timothy Pickering because he thought him well suited to tackle the challenges of Tunisian diplomacy.

Eaton's life had been marked by a stubborn determination. He had studied classical languages as a boy before, at age sixteen, running away to fight the British in the Revolution. After serving with a Connecticut regiment, he enrolled at Dartmouth College in 1785, but his scholarship was interrupted by winters spent teaching in country schools in order to earn his tuition money. At the end of one such break, he gathered his books, a change of clothes, and his tuition money into a small bundle he slung over his shoulder. He then set off on foot from the rural Connecticut town where he had been teaching, heading for Hanover, New Hampshire, nearly 150 miles north.

The summer of 1787 was unusually hot, and what Eaton had hoped would be a pleasant, if lengthy, journey on rustic trails through scenic countryside became a daunting slog along dusty roads overlooking fields choked by drought. Barely halfway to his destination, he found himself out of money, hungry, and still short of the New Hampshire border. But demonstrating the resourcefulness and adaptability he would display over and over in his life, he hit upon a solution. The only possessions he carried with him of any value were the pins and needles in his sewing kit. By selling the pins one at a time, he scraped together just enough to continue on the last miles to Hanover.

After graduation, Eaton returned to the army, gaining a captain's commission in 1792. Throughout his service—he would remain in the U.S. Army for five years—Captain Eaton would wrestle with his fiery temper and a tendency to take grievances personally. He narrowly avoided a duel with a fellow officer who accused him of disobeying an order. Only the intercession of other officers prevented an exchange of deadly fire, persuading the men to accept that both were culpable. "[After] Capt. B. conceded, and offered me his hand," Eaton noted in his journal, "[I] accepted it."[7] Honor—both personal and national—was a matter worth fighting for.

Eaton's reputation was for toughness; a skilled marksman, he could ride a horse all day and survive on his own wits when he had to. He spent time stationed at Fort Recovery, where he gained the respect of the legendary General Anthony Wayne. Known as "Mad Anthony" for his distinguished and fiercely committed service in General Washington's army, Wayne observed that "Eaton is firm in constitution as in resolution;—industrious, indefatigable, determined and persevering. . . . When in danger, he is in his element; and never shows to so good advantage, as when leading a charge."[8] A few years later, while stationed in swamps along the Georgia border with Spanish Florida, Eaton befriended the native tribes he had been sent to Georgia to fight. "I have frequently invited both Indians and traders to my quarters and entertained them," he wrote to an army official.[9] His unorthodox approach to frontier diplomacy aroused suspicions and irritated merchants in the region while his blunt appraisals of the campaign did not always sit well with his superiors. But Secretary of State Pickering liked what he saw. He valued Eaton's keen eye for reporting details, prompt correspondence, and gift for learning languages.

In January 1799, the new consuls made their first stop in North Africa at Algiers, where O'Brien was serving as consul to the dey, in addition to his duty as consul general. O'Brien greeted them warmly. With Cathcart's intimate knowledge of the region and Eaton's negotiating experience, O'Brien was optimistic that the new treaties could be preserved.

Eager to welcome them, O'Brien showed Cathcart and Eaton the city of Algiers. The densely packed streetscapes rose from a fortress at sea level into the hills that overlooked the Mediterranean, a place of bright sun but cooling sea breezes. After introducing his colleagues to the new dey of Algiers, hoping that the troubles would blow over, O'Brien wished them well as they sailed for their new postings.

O'Brien and Eaton initiated a lively correspondence from their cities some five hundred miles apart, discussing matters of diplomatic delicacy. O'Brien warned the new consul that the American Department of State took months to respond and had very little understanding of Barbary culture; instead, O'Brien urged Eaton to ignore irrelevant American instructions and instead to trust his instincts. Unfortunately, he would soon discover that America's purchased peace was more fragile than he'd realized. Despite having signed treaties with the United States of America, not all of the Barbary rulers would remain satisfied with the new status quo.

Jefferson's grave doubts about purchasing peace on the Barbary Coast were about to resurface. The United States' first war as a sovereign nation loomed. George Washington's decision to continue building warships even while paying for peace would prove wise when it became clear that the Barbary powers could not be trusted to keep their word.

CHAPTER 3

The Humiliation of the USS George Washington

I hope I shall never again be sent to Algiers with tribute, unless
I am authorized to deliver it from the mouth of our cannon.

—Captain William Bainbridge, USS *George Washington*

William Bainbridge shaded his eyes against the September sun glinting off the Mediterranean Sea. Standing on the deck of the USS *George Washington*, the six-foot-tall Bainbridge felt honored to command one of the first ships in America's navy—even if he was carrying tribute to a foreign power.

The new century had opened with treaties in place that mandated peace. But Bainbridge remained very much on the lookout. The secretary of the navy himself had ordered his young captain to be alert for any signs of "hostilities against the Vessels of the U: States" that might be committed by "the Barbary powers." Thus captain and crew stood ready, as instructed, to offer a fight in case O'Brien, Cathcart, and Eaton's peace was broken.

His broad features framed by his thick sideburns, the twenty-six-year-old Bainbridge understood his voyage was a historic one. No other American military vessel had ever passed through the Strait of Gibraltar flying the Stars and Stripes. Now, in 1800, he had the honor of advancing the reach of the young United States. Dwarfed by massive, rocky outcroppings jutting up from the sea, the *George Washington* had made history only days before by sailing through the famous strait. A stretch of sea less than nine miles wide between Europe and North Africa, the strait had figured in maritime lore since ancient times—the boundary between the Mediterranean and the wild, mysterious open ocean of the Atlantic to the west.

On approaching the North African coast, Bainbridge saw a blazing, burning desert that appeared to extend for days and weeks, reaching far into the largely unmapped African continent. This region, the Maghreb, as the natives called it, was ruled by the Barbary nations. Despite the proximity to the pirates' homeland, Bainbridge had seen no evidence of American shipping in trouble. So far his ship's log recorded only the sighting of two English frigates peaceably at anchor in the British port of Gibraltar and of a Danish brig on which all hands were "employed in scraping Decks."[1] The Barbary pirates seemed to be honoring the treaty that would be further secured once the *George Washington* delivered its cargo.

Captain Bainbridge was carrying a tribute payment to the Algerians, fulfilling the deal made by Barlow and O'Brien, but there was something different about this delivery. It was no accident that he commanded not a commercial vessel but an armed warship from the new U.S. Navy. As it sailed toward Algiers, the ship's presence served as a potent symbol. The USS *George Washington* was meant to convey that the United States was no longer a powerless, ragtag bunch of backwater settlements clinging to survival on the edge of the western Atlantic; they were growing, prospering states, independent in their industries, united under a central government—and possessed of a navy ready to act for the sake of the nation's interests and its self-defense.

If Bainbridge's ship wasn't intended as a direct threat, the USS *George Washington* was, at the very least, an implied promise that Americans would not bow to extortion forever.

Bainbridge was no run-of-the-mill ship's captain. He constantly found himself in the middle of controversy. After the teenaged Bainbridge signed on as an ordinary seaman aboard a merchant vessel, he helped put down a mutiny, suffering life-threatening injuries in the fight. When he recovered, the brave young man received command of his own merchant ship, from which he fired upon a much larger British vessel, causing enough damage for the enemy to surrender. At twenty-four he had joined the newly established U.S. Navy in 1798, rising rapidly from lieutenant to master commandant, despite a misadventure in which he was forced to surrender the schooner he commanded, having mistaken a powerful forty-gun French ship for a British frigate.

Now, Bainbridge's primary mission was to deliver tribute to Algiers—an uncomfortable task for a proud young sailor. He and his crew had watched carefully for pirate activity, but all was calm on the afternoon of September 17 as Algiers came into view. Bainbridge relaxed his guard, as the dey of Algiers was reportedly still friendly to the United States.

When the *George Washington* approached the harbor, the captain of the port of Algiers came aboard and, as was the custom,

Bainbridge entrusted him with the piloting of the ship through shoals and into the harbor. By evening, the USS *George Washington* was moored in the inner harbor, and the log noted that the crew had "got every thing Snug."[2]

Captain Bainbridge held his head high. He felt confident that he was operating from a position of strength, that he had executed his mission faithfully and unapologetically. He was prepared to salute Bobba Mustapha, dey of Algiers, and his city, and he expected that mutual respect would prevail in the soon-to-be-completed transaction.

He could hardly have been more wrong.

Boarding the ship along with the Algerian port pilot, Richard O'Brien had been the first American to greet Bainbridge and his men. As the U.S. consul general to Algiers, O'Brien had eagerly awaited the arrival of the *George Washington* for nearly four months. In a May 16 letter to the State Department, he had urgently requested that the government rush the overdue tribute to Algiers. Without the promised goods, he warned, "we cannot expect to preserve our affairs long."[3] If he was honest, he wasn't even sure that he would be able to keep the peace even if the tribute did arrive.

O'Brien's long experience in captivity gave him a deep understanding of how the Barbary bandits operated. Since at least the sixteenth century, the pirates had been turning over their booty to the nations' leaders to line their coffers. A portion of the profits were sent to Constantinople (today's Istanbul) as tribute to the Ottoman rulers, the recognized overlords of the Mohammedan world; a smaller portion went to the parties who made the capture; and the remainder became the property of the local ruler.

Captives were treated as if they, too, were goods. Men such as O'Brien and his crew were enslaved to local rulers or sold on the auction block to caravan owners, caliphs, and slave traders. Some of the more fortunate captives would be ransomed, usually for huge sums of money; a few would escape. But the only other option was to become a "renegade"—that is, to convert to Islam, because the Qur'an forbade the enslavement of Muslims by other Muslims. However, if a renegade was caught returning to his or her original faith upon emancipation, the penalty was death. Conversion was an option chosen by few—leaving most in captivity indefinitely.

European sailors were not the only slaves in the North African markets. There were women kidnapped from Russia and Syria to be bought and sold for harems or given as gifts to political leaders. There were other Africans, dark-skinned men and women from beyond the Sahara, transported across the desert by slave-trading caravans. Children as young as six, from Africa and Eastern Europe alike, were traded to work as serving boys or sexual slaves in bathhouses. Young men were forcibly converted to Islam and trained to guard the sultan.

Punishments for slaves were gruesome. Some captives reported witnessing castration, impaling, and the throwing of the offender off the city walls onto a series of hooks. Any Christian who insulted Islam could be subjected to severe punishment, including being burned alive. If a Christian man was found to be engaging in a relationship with a Muslim woman, he could be beheaded and his lover drowned. Should a Jew raise a hand against a Muslim, the hand could be cut off. The most common punishment, however, whatever the faith or national origin of the offender, was a beating.

Some of the luckier ones were elevated to the status of servants. A few served in the ruler's court; others served in the royal kitchens or worked in the dey's gardens, minding the plants and his menagerie of wild animals. No matter the assignment, however, the work remained hard and humiliating—especially for men and women from a country established upon the ideal of personal liberty.

While most of the other former American captives vowed never to return to the Barbary Coast, O'Brien had been treated relatively well during captivity, and he had been eager for the opportunity to work for peace between the governments. Yet on arriving at the docks in Algiers with Captain Bainbridge, O'Brien experienced a renewed feeling of powerlessness. The hold of the *George Washington* contained only a few of the articles that the dey expected, and delivery of the promised gold and silver had been delayed. After O'Brien explained the facts, Bainbridge too understood that he had arrived in a tinderbox—and it wasn't only a matter of hot, dry air and burning sun.

BOXED IN

The next day, the crew of the USS *George Washington* began unloading the dey's tribute, which included oak planks and pine, along with boxes of tin and casks of nails. The weather was pleasant and the winds gentle, and the men prepared to take aboard fresh stores of grapes, green figs, oranges, and almonds as well. Unaware of the diplomatic tension, the sailors aboard the *George Washington* expected that, having completed delivery as ordered, their ship would depart promptly for the return journey to their home port of Philadelphia.

But the "despotic dey," as Bainbridge soon referred to him, had other plans for them.

In keeping with custom, the American captain, accompanied by O'Brien, sought an audience with the Algerian ruler to pay his respects. As the crew discharged the cargo back in the harbor, Captain Bainbridge, Consul O'Brien, and the Algerian minister of the harbor met the dey at his palace to give account of the tribute the Americans had brought. Dressed in flowing robes, his face half obscured by his generous beard, the aging dey grew angry upon learning that the ship had failed to bring all of the promised annuities.

"You pay me tribute," Bobba Mustapha declared. "By that, you become my slaves. I have, therefore, a right to order you as I may think proper."[4]

The outraged ruler then issued an order: he decreed that the USS *George Washington* must carry his ambassador and his entourage to the other end of the Mediterranean Sea to Constantinople, the capital of the Ottoman empire, where the dey's own annual tribute was due.

Bainbridge balked. He told his host that the assignment was impossible, as he had no orders to perform such a mission. O'Brien pointed out that the existing treaty permitted merchant vessels, but not military ships, to perform such duties for the Algerian regency. But even as they resisted, both of the Americans understood that they would have to obey. As O'Brien admitted a day later in a letter intended for the eyes of the secretary of state, "I am afraid [we] shall be obliged to give way to prevent extraordinary difficulties."[5]

What he did not explain was why the *George Washington* could not simply ignore the dey, weigh anchor, and set sail for home: On arrival in what he'd believed was a safe harbor, the gullible Bainbridge had permitted the Algerian pilot to direct the ship to a berth directly beneath the guns of the fortress, a huge tactical error. Overly trusting, Bainbridge did not consider how his ship would make its exit should the talks with the dey go poorly, and now it was too late. Dwarfed by the fortification, the vessel faced two hundred cannons and a fleet of armed Algerian ships. Moored within range of the Algerian batteries, the USS *George Washington* was hopelessly outgunned and outmanned. If Bainbridge and his men attempted to escape, their ship could easily be blasted to kindling if the dey so ordered.

Bainbridge was out of options. The only way to send a message back to the Department of the Navy was by another ship, and ships from the Mediterranean, sailing against the prevailing westerly winds, often took two months to reach the United States and another month or more to return. In the event of severe weather, the turnaround time could be even longer, and the dey wasn't going to wait several months. Entrusted with both his ship and the honor of his country, Bainbridge had to make a decision on his own.

In the coming days, Bainbridge continued to argue that he could not comply with the humiliating request. But the dey's anger deepened. He demanded payment of what O'Brien calculated was "upwards of 110 thousand dollars in debt."[6] The regency's ruler escalated his threats, warning that, if Bainbridge failed to perform the mission, friendly relations between their nations would come to an end and Algerian corsairs would again harass shipping as they had done in the past. It was a threat that O'Brien, the former captain of the captured *Dauphin,* understood very well.

Bainbridge could do little but watch as other ships departed while he remained at the dey's mercy. He supervised sail repairs, and his ship's log recorded the weather and the activity of his crew. Finally, after several weeks of demands and demurrals as the

Americans and Algerians went back and forth, O'Brien received a final summons. He was told that Bainbridge must submit to the order or surrender the ship and subject his crew to captivity. A refusal, O'Brien understood, would also have a wider consequence: it would mean war with Algiers. With no alternative, the two Americans bowed to the dey's demand.

What had begun as a proud voyage was about to become a national disgrace. As Bainbridge observed sternly to O'Brien, "Sir, I cannot help observing that the event of this day makes me ponder on the words Independent United States."[7]

A FLOATING ZOO

The humiliation of the USS *George Washington* began. Only after agreeing to transport the ambassador did Bainbridge learn the extent of the diplomatic retinue. This would be no modest delegation, but the ship, configured for a maximum crew of 220 men, would be required to accommodate the ambassador, 100 attendants, plus 100 captive Africans.

The *George Washington* had become a slave ship.

The dey further required that the overloaded ship carry gifts bound for his ruler at Constantinople, including 4 horses, 25 cattle, and 150 sheep, in addition to 4 lions, 4 tigers, 4 antelopes, and 12 parrots.[8]

The warship had become a floating zoo.

Then, just before departure, adding another insult to the cramped quarters, the deafening squawking, and the stench of manure, the dey's coup de grâce fell. He ordered the American flag taken down and the Algerine flag hoisted. Seven guns were fired in salute of the new flag. Among the American crew, the ship's log recorded, "some tears fell at this Instance of national Humility."[9]

The USS *George Washington* had become a Barbary ferry service.

The journey to Constantinople took twenty-three days. Once in open water and out of range of the harbor guns, Bainbridge raised his own flag, unopposed by the Algerians on board. Yet he wasn't truly in control of his own ship, as the uninvited passengers demanded that the ship's course be adapted to their prayer schedule. The helmsman was forced to navigate so that the *George Washington,* though pushing its way through stormy seas, pointed eastward toward Mecca five times a day for the faithful to perform their required prayers. One of the Muslims was assigned to watch the compass heading to ensure the correctness of the ship's position.

While the American crew found a certain dark humor in this peculiar manner of worship, the situation was no laughing matter. The trip was uncomfortable and degrading—and it would have serious diplomatic repercussions. When the *George Washington* deposited its haul in Constantinople and turned homeward, Captain Bainbridge remarked, his resolve firm, "I hope I shall never again be sent to Algiers with tribute, unless I am authorized to deliver it from the mouth of our cannon."

When the ship finally returned to the United States, the American public was outraged by the report. As news of the events in Algiers spread, some regarded Bainbridge's submission as inexcusable. Many believed that the United States had stared evil in the face and blinked first. Others complained that it had been blinking for years and that to continue to pay tribute was to invite more abuse. Those against the navy also felt justified; the attempt to demonstrate that the

United States possessed military might in international waters had backfired. The USS *George Washington* had been unable to prevent its own hijacking.

On learning of the events at Algiers, William Eaton, stationed at Tunis, gave vent to his strong feelings in writing to his fellow diplomat Richard O'Brien.

> *History shall tell that the United States first volunteer'd a ship of war, equipt, a carrier for a pirate—It is written— Nothing but blood can blot the impression out—Frankly I own, I would have lost the piece, and been myself impaled rather than yielded this concession.*[10]

Horrified by America's inaction in the face of the humiliation, Eaton added a final question: "Will nothing rouse my country?"

CHAPTER 4

Jefferson Takes Charge

I will wait Six months for an Answer to my letter to the President . . . if it does not arrive in that period . . . I will declare war in form against the United States.

—**Yusuf Qaramanli, bashaw of Tripoli, October 1800**

While William Bainbridge and the *George Washington* suffered humiliation abroad, Americans at home were in turmoil over the election of the nation's third president. After a bitter contest that threatened the unity of the new nation, Thomas Jefferson had beaten his friend John Adams and was inaugurated on March 4, 1801. Deeply disappointed and angry at his former companion, Adams did not attend the inauguration.

An estranged friend and a divided nation were not Jefferson's only problems. He would now have to face the problem of the Barbary powers head-on. For more than a dozen years, the nation's policy under both Presidents Washington and Adams had been to avoid resorting to military force. But Jefferson would soon learn that time had run out.

WAR AND PEACE

Unaware that the ticking time bomb of the Barbary Coast was about to go off, Jefferson settled gradually into his new home. After his walk to the Capitol for his inauguration, the third president let two full weeks pass before he moved from his rented rooms into the president's quarters.

Occupying only a few rooms on the main floor, Jefferson began to plan the social life of the place. Unlike Washington and Adams, who hosted weekly presidential receptions as if at a royal court, Jefferson preferred smaller dinners where the business of the government might get done in intimate conversations. But those would come later. First he needed to gain a fuller understanding of the state in which Adams had left various matters.

President Jefferson ordered that all correspondence be submitted to him for review. As he looked over the papers Adams had left behind, his concern about the state of America's safety grew. Jefferson had known the Barbary situation was bad, but he hadn't realized how bad it truly was. Now, as he reviewed the existing treaties with Algiers, Tripoli, and Tunis. The last had been ratified in January 1800 and promised payment of $20,000 in annual tribute, as well as the bizarre payment of one barrel of gunpowder every time an American vessel received a cannon salute. After fifteen years of observation, Jefferson knew as well as anyone that this demand was not in good faith. Instead, it was a warning that the whole region was nothing less than a powder keg.

On March 13, a stack of fresh dispatches from the Mediterranean had arrived for Jefferson's review. One in particular, from James Cathcart, had about it the whiff of a burning fuse. Writing before the *George Washington* had been commandeered, Cathcart reported that the bashaw of Tripoli had increased a demand in his annual tribute, despite the provision in the treaty stating that no "periodical tribute or farther payment is ever to be made by either party."[1] That, Cathcart reported, was of no matter whatever to the regent.

As Jefferson read on, Cathcart's long and detailed letter grew more ominous. The bashaw's rising rhetoric had turned to explicit threats. "Let your government give me a sum of money & I will be content—but I will be paid one way or the other." The bashaw set a six-month deadline, after which, if his demands were not met? "I will declare war . . . against the United States." Those six months were nearly up.

Jefferson also found a letter from Tunis consul William Eaton. Sensing that the fragile peace would not last, Eaton had begged Adams's administration to make a show of strength. He proposed sending three of America's most impressive fighting ships into Tripoli. There he would invite the bashaw to dinner and impress him with the Americans' strength. After the meal, he would point at the cannon and say, "See there our *executive power* Commissioned to Keep Guarentee of Peace."[2] If the plan worked, Eaton explained, the bashaw might be too intimidated to declare war.

Unfortunately, one of Adams's last acts in office had been to sign into law a bill shrinking the American navy. Jefferson must have sympathized with Eaton, whose plan resembled Jefferson's own from years earlier, but there were few ships to send. Jefferson did not have enough military power to take America properly to war.

A few weeks later, he learned that his time to weigh options had run out. The USS *George Washington* docked at Philadelphia on April 19. After completing their humiliating journey to Constantinople, William Bainbridge and his crew had endured a punishing winter passage home. The stormy Atlantic journey took two and a half months, twice the usual transit time. Still, the long trip and cold winds had done nothing to lessen Bainbridge's red-hot fury and, back on dry land, he set off immediately to the nation's capital to give the president a full report.

The city of Washington was full of whispered criticism of Bainbridge, as some hinted that he'd capitulated too easily to the dey's demands. But the captain found a sympathetic ear in President Jefferson. Fully aware of the region's problems, Jefferson was predisposed to believe that Bainbridge's situation had been impossible. Once he'd heard the details from Bainbridge directly, the president saw to it that Bainbridge was commended for "the able and judicious manner in which he had discharged his duty under such peculiarly embarrassing circumstances."[3] He contemplated a further reward to the dedicated captain—perhaps he might return to the Barbary Coast, this time in a vessel more intimidating than a converted merchant ship.

First, though, Jefferson needed to convene his cabinet. He wanted to secure their approval of a plan that was taking shape in his mind—a plan that would fall somewhere between submitting to the Barbary indignities and launching a full-scale war.

Jefferson had hoped to gather his cabinet in Washington by the end of April, but it was mid-May before they assembled. Washington's main newspaper, the *National Intelligencer and Daily Advertiser*, had proclaimed just four days earlier that the nation was at peace, but Jefferson and his advisers knew better. The situation on the Barbary Coast demanded action, even though everyone at the table also understood that the United States was among the least qualified of nation states to take on pirates with its small navy, which was shrinking further even as they took their seats.

Jefferson put the question boldly, asking his advisers at this, his first cabinet meeting: "Shall the squadron now at Norfolk be ordered to cruise in the Mediterranean?"[4]

The gentlemen of the cabinet immediately recognized the question had broad significance: they were being asked to consider whether the president's authority extended to take military action without first gaining permission from Congress.

With the question before the cabinet, Jefferson, as he often did, noted on a sheet of paper the opinions of each official.

Secretary of the Treasury Albert Gallatin expressed the opinion that "the Executive can not put us in a state of war." But, he added, in the event of war, whether declared by Congress or initiated by another country, "the command and direction of the public force then belongs to the Executive."

Attorney General Levi Lincoln was still more measured: "Our men of war may repel an attack," he said, "but after the repulse, may not proceed to destroy the enemy's vessels."

Secretary of War Henry Dearborn took a more bullish view. "The expedition should go forward openly to protect our commerce against the threatened hostilities of Tripoli," he offered. Secretary of State Madison concurred.

After further discussion, the cabinet was unanimous: the

squadron would be dispatched to the Mediterranean but as peacemakers rather than agents of war.[5] Jefferson and his cabinet hoped against hope that the Barbary powers would be reasonable, would recognize that the United States took seriously the seizure of its goods and citizens, and would back down from the conflict.

Richard Dale, one of the original U.S. Navy captains appointed by George Washington, was named to command the squadron. He would carry with him a letter from President Jefferson, addressed to the leader of Tripoli; in its text, Jefferson offered multiple assurances of "constant friendship."

Jefferson chose his words carefully, avoiding inflammatory terms such as *warship*. He advised the bashaw that "we have found it expedient to detach a *squadron of observation* into the Mediterranean." To the careful reader, however, the words were rich with implications: the Americans did not appreciate the Barbary Coast's treatment of their ships, but they were not yet ready to go to war. With any luck, simply letting the Muslim leaders know they were being watched would be enough to dissuade them.

"We hope [our ships'] appearance will give umbrage to no Power," Jefferson's letter continued, "for, while we mean to rest the safety of our commerce on the resources of our own strength & bravery in every sea, we have yet given to this squadron in strict command to conduct themselves toward all friendly Powers with most perfect respect and good order."

President Jefferson could only hope that his words of peace, accompanied by a modest show of power, would quiet the visions of war that danced in the mind of the bashaw of Tripoli.

CHAPTER 5

A Flagpole Falls

Facts are now indubitable. The Bashaws corsaires are actually out and fitting out against Americans.

—William Eaton to the secretary of state, April 10, 1801

While Jefferson and his cabinet prepared a response to Barbary provocation, James Cathcart stood in a diplomatic no-man's-land. For almost six months he had waited impatiently for a response from Washington to his October 1800 letter outlining the war threats from Tripolitan bashaw Yusuf Qaramanli. No instructions came. He didn't even know who had won the presidential election. For all intents and purposes, Cathcart was alone.

Over the past few months, the bashaw had alternatively threatened and flattered the United States. He had told Cathcart he wanted peace with his people, but refused to discuss the existing treaty, still legally in effect. The bashaw simply wanted more and didn't pretend otherwise, whatever he had agreed to in the past. He first demanded a gift of ships—the other regencies had gotten more in their treaties, he pointed out, in particular Algiers. Now he insisted upon further considerations, too. The bashaw demanded immense amounts of money, including a down payment of $225,000, far more than Cathcart could give or the U.S. Treasury could afford. He was entirely shameless in his demands, having had the audacity to demand an additional $10,000 in tribute when George Washington died. The bashaw, in short, was living up to the prediction made by Joel Barlow years before. The Tripolitan ruler was willing to set aside "every principle of honor at defiance more than any prince in Barbary."[1] As far as the Americans could tell, he was the worst of a bad lot.

His fear rising, Cathcart had issued a circular letter to his fellow consuls on February 21, 1801. "I am convinced that the Bashaw of Tripoli," he warned, "will commence Hostilitys against the U. States of America in less than Sixty Days."[2]

He was not far off; his fears were confirmed on May 11, 1801, three months later.

At six o'clock that Monday evening, a regency emissary arrived at the American consulate in Tripoli. When the visitor was ushered in, Cathcart immediately recognized the man as one of Bashaw Yusuf's most esteemed advisers. Cathcart greeted him with all the cordiality he could muster, which had never been much. He had done his best to remain patient with the bashaw's games, but his patience with masked aggression was wearing thin.

This time, the bashaw's emissary didn't even pretend to come in peace. He delivered his message. "The Bashaw has sent me to inform you that he has declared war against the United States and will take down your flagstaff on Thursday the 14th."[3]

The bashaw had made many threats in the past, but Cathcart understood this one was real. Tripolitan ships, in a gesture of contempt, had already raised the American colors in the place where they flew the flags of nations at war with the regency. This time there was nothing Cathcart could do to defuse the situation.

His instincts told him he must leave; he knew that the bashaw would allow him to vacate the city. But Cathcart had grown accustomed to this overgrown village that rose from the sea, its long wharf extending far into the harbor. The walled city, with the minarets of its mosques reaching high above the tightly packed stone houses, had become his home. Even the labyrinths of the bashaw's palace, situated at the highest point of the city, had become dear to him in some strange way.

Though he would always remain an outsider, Carthcart understood this world. He had sat cross-legged to share a dinner with the bashaw. He knew the odors of the main squares of the city, thick with the scent of rich coffee and tobacco smoke. He recognized the sounds of camels in harness, turning the shafts of the city's flour mill. The sight of slaves fanning their masters, driving away the flies, was familiar if unwelcome. Like it or not, the city had become part of him, and now, as he had feared, it was spitting him out.

Holding both his temper and his sorrow in check, Cathcart replied politely to the bashaw's emissary, knowing that an angry reply would only jeopardize his wife and young daughter, as well as his diplomatic staff. Without instructions from the government at home, he was authorized to do nothing else. And even if he could know the new president's mind, military backup would never reach him in time. Accordingly, Cathcart acknowledged receipt of the declaration of war and said he would charter a ship and depart the city as soon as possible. In the meantime, he would remain at the consulate and witness the first official act of war.

A TRIPOLITAN TRAGICOMEDY

Three days later, the bashaw made good on his threat. On May 14, 1801, he dispatched his men to the American consulate; the party of soldiers arrived at one o'clock that Thursday afternoon.

Cathcart was ready to make one last offer to keep the peace, to avoid what had begun to seem inevitable. He approached the *seraskier*, the leader of the squad and the bashaw's minister of war, and asked that the promise of a tribute of $10,000 be conveyed to the bashaw. A messenger departed for the castle, but returned minutes later. The bashaw had rejected the offer.

Cathcart knew any further attempts at diplomacy would be futile, and stopping the bashaw's men by force was impossible. Helpless, he stood watching on that bright, hot Thursday as the Tripolitans began hacking at the flagpole.

The bashaw's men shouted encouragement to one another as they swung their axes but to their dismay, felling the pole was harder than it looked. Chips flew, but the flagpole refused to fall. As if to mock the men, the flag fluttered with each stroke of the ax, its staff staunchly in place. A gesture meant to humble the Americans was rapidly becoming a humiliation for the Tripolitans.

The bashaw had ordered that, if the men had trouble dropping the pole, they should pull on the halyard, the line anchored at the top of the pole used to hoist the flag. He thought they might be able to break the pole in half by doing so. To the dismay of the men, that strategy failed, too, and once again, the resilient flagpole refused to fall. The men who had arrived to dishonor the flag were proving singularly inept.

More than an hour passed before the Tripolitans finally caused the pole to splinter just enough to lean against the consulate house. The American diplomats looked on, darkly amused by the whole episode. Cathcart wryly recorded the events in a dispatch to Secretary of State James Madison.

"At a quarter past two they effected the grand atchievement and our Flagstaff was chop'd down six feet from the ground & left reclining on the Terrace. . . . Thus ends the first act of this Tragedy."[4]

AMERICA AT WAR

Ten days would pass before Cathcart, his wife, and his daughter sailed out of Tripoli harbor aboard a polacca, a small three-masted ship he hired in the harbor. He entrusted the consulate affairs he left behind to the good hands of the Danish consul general, Nicholas Nissen. Cathcart specifically instructed that any American sailors brought captive to Tripoli be provided for with money for subsistence and needed medical care. Nissen agreed to do whatever was in his power to meet those needs should another American ship be captured.[5]

The fleeing family landed at Malta three days later. There Cathcart gave letters for the American government to a ship that would convey them homeward. He still had no idea who was president or what the political climate was in the United States. He could only imagine what the response would be when the documents reached America.

Once state business was taken care of, the Cathcarts' vessel made sail again, headed for the Italian city of Leghorn. But now-former consul Cathcart's tribulations were not yet at an end. Off the coast of Sicily he had another unwelcome encounter with a Barbary force, this one a small Tunisian ship manned by pirates. They proved respectful of Cathcart's credentials, although he had his "trunks tumbled" and the boarders helped themselves to his wine and food-stuffs. Mrs. Cathcart and her daughter had been terrified at the appearance of a man in their cabin wielding a saber, but the Tunisian employed the weapon, Cathcart reported, "not with any intention to hurt any person but merely to cut twine & other ligatures which were round the articles he plunder'd."[6]

The pirates having helped themselves to the ship's compass, Cathcart and the captain were forced to resort to paste and ceiling wax to repair "an old french Compas whose needle fortunately retain'd its magentism." It proved adequate for charting their course, and the Cathcarts managed to make Leghorn nine days after departing Tripoli. On arrival, however, one last insult was delivered: they faced a twenty-five-day quarantine to ensure they had not contracted smallpox or any other diseases in their encounter with the Tunisians.

Once they were ashore in Italy, the news finally reached Cathcart of Jefferson's election. He sent his congratulations, via a letter to Madison, who along with Jefferson would remain unaware for many more weeks that Tripoli had declared war. Jefferson would learn of Tripoli's attack too late to assist Cathcart, who was already traveling home. But thanks to Jefferson's foresight, American ships had already been ordered to head for the Barbary Coast. They were not authorized to attack the Barbary ships, but they would be able to defend American interests against further embarrassment and blockade Barbary ports, squeezing Tripoli's economy the same way the pirates had been squeezing America's. Both nations knew that a breaking point had been reached, but neither side knew that the other had taken action.

CHAPTER 6

The First Flotilla

I hope the next Opportunity that I have of writing you, that
I shall have the pleasure of Informing you that some of the
Squadron has made some Captures of the Tripolitan Corsairs.

—Richard Dale to the secretary of the navy, July 19, 1801

A n ocean away from Cathcart's splintered flagpole, Jefferson's four warships prepared for their voyage. The flagship
would be the *President*, commanded by Commodore
Richard Dale. The *Philadelphia* and the *Essex*, captained by Samuel
Barron and William Bainbridge, respectively, would add additional
strength. A fourth vessel, the trim schooner *Enterprise*, guided by
Lieutenant Andrew Sterett, completed the flotilla. Though modest
in numbers, the flotilla was surprisingly powerful due to a new design. Because of innovations in American shipbuilding, the American frigates would be able to outrun much larger ships or, in heavy
seas, match up with them.

Adding to the military might of the four ships were members of the relatively new United States Marine Corps, reactivated by President Adams with the birth of the U.S. Navy in 1798. Skilled combatants, the Marines were invaluable during boarding actions and landing expeditions, and they also served to protect a ship's officers in the event of a mutiny by the crew. The fighters had a reputation for being bold, fearless men—though sometimes a little brash and reckless. Their presence would be invaluable should any of Dale's ships encounter pirates or need protection on land.

Once fully provisioned, Dale's squadron finally made sail for the Strait of Gibraltar on June 2, 1801. Soon after losing sight of the American coast, they met with rough seas. Swirling squalls made the first ten days of the crossing difficult, as easterly winds and heavy rains buffeted the ships. As the newest of the four American vessels, the USS *President* had only a few months of sailing to her credit, and the storms found every flaw in her construction. Wracked by the thrashing of the sea, she soon had rain and seawater leaking through seams that opened in her deck. Life below became damp and unpleasant, and many of the crew fell seasick. But she was a fine ship, from the top of her three tall masts to her bottom. A little stormy weather would not prevent the USS *President* from reaching her Mediterranean destination.

JEFFERSON'S COMMANDERS

The *President*'s commander was no less sturdy. At forty-five years of age, Richard Dale's portly bearing, kind eyes, and crown of graying hair hinted at the maturity of long experience that he brought to his command. He had gone to sea at age twelve, and after making his first

Atlantic crossing aboard a merchant vessel owned by an uncle, he worked himself up to the rank of mate by age seventeen.

During the American Revolution, Dale served as John Paul Jones's second-in-command aboard the converted French merchant ship USS *Bon Homme Richard*. Swinging by a rope under a moonlight sky, he had been the first American sailor to land on the deck of the HMS *Serapis* during a battle with the British ship, an act of bravery that won him widespread fame. After the war he settled for a quieter life, establishing a profitable merchant business based on trade with China and India. When the U.S. Navy was reestablished, however, Dale had been quick to accept President Washington's offer to return to the sea as one of its first captains. While a sense of duty drove the men aboard the American ships, Commodore Dale understood firsthand the need to protect American ships from capture—he himself had been imprisoned by the British during the Revolution.

Aboard the USS *Essex*, Captain Bainbridge had been chosen to go back to the region where he had suffered his degrading experience aboard the *George Washington*, and revenge was on his mind. But there were younger men about the *Essex* with simpler motives, among them the lust for adventure. Lieutenant Stephen Decatur was one.

Every now and then, fate seems to smile on an individual, gifting him with an extraordinary measure of good looks, character, and opportunity. Stephen Decatur's curly dark hair, sparkling eyes, and devil-may-care attitude caught the eye of many a woman when he entered a room. But his bravery—known to verge on recklessness— and his intense sense of honor were equally distinguishing features.

Once, when a British merchant insulted Decatur and the American navy, Decatur challenged him to a duel. Knowing his pistol skills were far superior to his foe's, Decatur confessed to a friend that he planned only to shoot for the man's leg, hoping to wound him slightly and teach him a lesson. The duel went as Decatur had planned. The Englishman missed entirely and Decatur's bullet went into the man's hip, rather than his heart. Decatur sustained no injury and his pride was satisfied. He did not want to kill the man, but he could not let the slur pass unpunished. To insult the U.S. Navy was to insult Decatur, his country, and his family.

The sea had been a part of Decatur's life for as long as he could remember. His father, Stephen Decatur Sr., had served as a naval captain in the Revolution before becoming a successful merchant. When his eight-year-old son and namesake had come down with a case of whooping cough, the doctors prescribed a regimen of sea air to help clear the recovering child's lungs, so the boy joined his father on his next voyage. When he returned from the trip to Europe, the young Decatur was cured of his cough—but freshly infected with a desire for the nautical life. Despite his mother's dearest hope that he would join the clergy, he left college after one year to pursue a naval career.

Even in the face of the stormy conditions of June 1801, Lieutenant Decatur counted himself the luckiest of men to have a place on this mission. Every creak of the frigate as she rocked on the waves whispered of glory ahead. The salty air filling his lungs gave him an invigorating sense of the honor of simply being an American—a child not of old borders and ancient alliances, but of ideals and liberty. And he took pride in his ship; although the *Essex* was smaller than the *President*, Decatur felt a swelling of pride as he considered the line of cannons, more than thirty in all.

Neither he nor any of the sailors in the four-ship fleet had any way of knowing what was brewing in Tripoli. They had their suspicions, of course, and Commodore Dale had provided Bainbridge with orders in case they should encounter hostilities. If the *Essex* should get separated as they crossed the Atlantic, Dale instructed, Bainbridge and Decatur and their men should head for Gibraltar. If they learned there that the Barbary states had declared war, they were to wait five days. If the remaining ships failed to arrive within that window, Bainbridge was to leave a message for Dale with the American consul and then proceed into the Mediterranean to provide protective escort for American merchant ships. In the event that war had not been declared, the *Essex* was to wait twenty days for the other ships before departing to carry out its mission, leaving a letter at every port of call so that Dale could trace her.

Dale's detailed orders covered other matters, too. Professional decorum and propriety were stressed, and the commodore's orders for gallantry suited young Lieutenant Decatur just fine. He was confident, handsome, and brave. He was setting off on a grand voyage for the honor of his country to an exotic place he had only ever dreamed of visiting. If there was peace, let it be lasting; if there was war, then let it be swift and decisive—and let him be bold in the heat of battle and bring honor, esteem, and victory to his country. Whatever lay ahead on the Barbary Coast, Stephen Decatur was certain it would be a great adventure.

RULES OF ENGAGEMENT

When Dale's ships emerged from the gales, the commodore began running his men through cannon drills. Each man had a precise role in the exercises, and soon the air was filled with orders—"Level your guns" . . . "Take off your tompions" . . . "Load with cartridge" . . .

"Shot your guns" . . . "Fire!" With a deafening roar, cannonball shot flew hundreds of yards before disappearing into the waves.

The captains were training their men, veteran and novice alike, for a kind of warfare peculiar to the Barbary Coast. There would be no lines of battle, with opposing enemy fleets facing off. When attacking, Barbary ships closed rapidly, their first strategy to board their opponent. Thus the best defense for a ship under Barbary attack was coordinated cannon fire to keep the pirates at a distance.

To Dale's frustration, though, a good defense was all he was authorized to do. Beginning with the debate in his cabinet in Washington two and a half months before, President Jefferson hesitated to claim with certainty that he had the constitutional right to declare war. Thus, the orders transmitted down the line of command—via

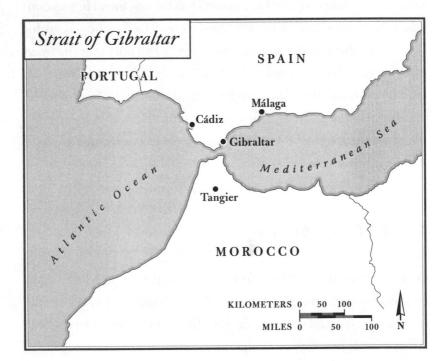

the secretary of the navy, to Commodore Dale, and on to his captains—were abundantly clear. "Should you fall in with any of the Tripolitan Corsairs . . . on your passage to Malta," Dale wrote, ". . . you will heave all his Guns Over board Cut away his Masts, & leave him In a situation, that he can Just make out to get into some Port."[1] American ships were not to capture any Barbary ships. They could hobble ships that attacked them, but they were to take no captives and to let their enemies escape.

Fortunately, American guns were fired only in practice during the journey across the Atlantic, and the USS *President* sailed into Gibraltar on July 2. The imposing frigate was followed by the smaller *Philadelphia* and the *Essex*. The fourth ship, the *Enterprise*, greeted her. The heavy seas off North America had slowed the *Enterprise* and, rather than slow the pace of his little fleet, Commodore Dale permitted the sloop to break company. Once the weather cleared, however, Lieutenant Sterett had set a speedy pace en route to Gibraltar and actually beat the other ships by five days.

The fleet may have been modest by the standards of Europe's largest navies, but the four warships of the United States made an impressive showing. Whether they would be able to secure peace was not yet known, but for the first time, a flotilla of American warships would make anchor in a Mediterranean port.

PIRATES IN PORT

On arrival at Gibraltar, Commodore Richard Dale's first duty was to find out the status of the fragile Barbary peace. But first, he wanted to settle into the harbor.

The harbor was emptier than usual. Gibraltar was home to a Royal Navy base, but all of the British ships, engaged in the war with Napoleon, a conflict that the Americans hoped to avoid, had been sent out to blockade French and Spanish forces. On spotting the USS *Enterprise* at anchor in the nearly vacant harbor, Dale made to join her, relieved that Lieutenant Sterett and his men had arrived safely, with no apparent harm to their vessel. The American squadron had been reunited.

As his ship neared the American schooner, however, Dale's attention was drawn to another vessel moored nearby. It was unlike any he had ever seen.

The ship's stern sat unusually low in the water, but it was the brightly colored hull that caught Dale's eye. As the *President* neared, Dale saw that the yellow two-masted ship, a white stripe running its length, carried many guns. A closer look with a spyglass revealed she was heavily manned, her crew much larger than normal for a ship her size.

He also noted that the ship was not alone. A second, smaller vessel accompanied her, a brig armed with fourteen guns. Both ships were elaborately painted with festoons of flowers, but the larger ship had a much more disconcerting ornament: a woman's severed head suspended above the deck.

These were pirate ships, Dale knew in an instant—most likely from Tripoli.

The presence of Barbary ships made Dale uneasy, but he didn't fear an attack. Whether a state of war existed or not, he knew neither side would open fire within the confines of a neutral harbor. Even if the two garishly painted ships were foolish enough to try, they would be no match for his firepower.

As his ship glided toward its mooring, Dale looked upon the larger of the two vessels—it bore the name *Meshuda*—and the unnamed brig. There, rocking gently in the harbor swell, lay the answer he was looking for. The Tripolitan commander of this little fleet would know whether a state of war existed between their countries.

Commodore Dale decided all he had to do was ask; whether the pirate would give him a straight answer remained to be seen.

If the *Meshuda* seemed familiar to the Americans, it was because she had once been an American ship, known as the *Betsey,* but captured by Tripolitan pirates five years earlier. Her crew had been taken captive, but all had been quickly released—except for one.

Along with the ship, a single deckhand stayed behind when his shipmates sailed for home. He did so by choice. Born in the Scots port of Perth, the fair-haired and bearded Peter Lisle had turned renegade.

Bolstered by his fluency in Arabic acquired on earlier voyages, the deckhand quickly converted to Islam and abandoned his Christian name, adopting the name Murat Rais in honor of a great sixteenth-century Ottoman admiral. Over time, Peter-Lisle-turned-Murat Rais won the trust of the bashaw, even marrying the bashaw's daughter. Abandoning loyalties to his own king and country, he became a feared and cunning pirate, and he was now the captain of the renamed *Betsey,* the flagship of the Tripolitan fleet.

When Rais and his men had arrived at Gibraltar on June 29, 1801, they paid no mind to the *Enterprise*, already three days in port, but the appearance in Gibraltar Bay of the three American frigates on July 1 represented trouble on the horizon. Rais knew that his country had declared war on America. *But did the Americans know about the war?*

Rais realized these tall ships were not a direct response to the flagpole incident; that news could not have reached American shores in time to prompt the dispatch of this fleet. Yet with rumors of war rapidly crisscrossing the streets and market stalls of Gibraltar, Rais wondered how soon the men of these great fighting ships would learn of the sawed-off staff and the defiling of the American flag. And because the American government could not yet be aware of the declaration of war from Tripoli, just what were these warships doing in Mediterranean waters?

Watching the American sailors securing their ships at anchor, High Admiral Murat Rais devised a plan. He would feign ignorance once the Americans sought him out, as they were sure to do. He would not be the one to deliver the word of war.

UNANSWERED QUESTIONS

Before approaching the pirate ship to ask about the state of the peace, Dale decided to ask friendlier powers for information first. The U.S. consul to Gibraltar came aboard to welcome the fleet, but he had no information. Dale went ashore to pay his respects to the British governor, who confirmed the *Meshuda*'s loyalties and history, but he also had no answers.[2]

Dale would have to ask the pirate commander—and his 392 men.

The *Meshuda* and the brig were in quarantine (the Gibraltar Health Office wanted to be certain they did not carry disease), but Dale approached within hailing distance. Portly but imposing, his voice amplified by a hailing trumpet, he called out to Murat Rais. "The Comodor made Enquiry of the admiral," the U.S. consul noted, describing the exchange: "were they at War or Peace with the U. States?"[3]

From the deck of the *Meshuda*, Murat Rais replied—in the King's English—that they were at peace.

A doubtful Dale tried another tack. He inquired after Consul Cathcart. On departing Tripoli, had the American seemed well?

The reply was a surprise. A fortnight before, said Rais, Cathcart had gone from Tripoli.

Why?

Rais responded that Cathcart *"was no friend to the Americans."*

After this odd piece of news, Dale was able to extract nothing further. The exchange left Dale no less perplexed than when it began.

As for Murat Rais, he was under no illusions that he had fooled Commodore Dale, but his years in the Maghreb had taught him the art of deception. His adopted home was a place where one felt bound to dicker over the price of fruit in the market. Small scenes of drama—indignation, refusal, acceptance—unfolded before the purchase of a string of figs. When it came to the elaborate rituals of diplomacy, it was essential to act as if both parties were old friends, each concerned first and foremost with the comfort and reassurance of the other. To jump straight to the point was rude and disrespectful. It was also dangerous. To have admitted at the outset in his exchange with the American that their nations were at war would have been paramount to surrender.

For Dale, what he learned in the town—if not from Murat Rais—enabled him to reach one firm resolve. Charged by Jefferson and the secretary of the navy to safeguard American ships in the Mediterranean, Dale could not take the other man's word. Instead he had to make a judgment based upon the scraps of intelligence he had gathered, as well as upon his well-honed instincts. "From every information that I can get here Tripoli is at war with America," he reported. That meant he had to act.

He set about issuing orders. The *Essex* was to take under convoy the merchant ship *Grand Turk*, readying to sail for Tunis, its hold full of naval stores and other goods as tribute. There were relationships with other Barbary states to be maintained.

Dale learned that more than two dozen American vessels at nearby Barcelona awaited escort, as did many other merchantmen at other ports of call along the southern European coast. He instructed Bainbridge, after completing his errand to Tunis, that the *Essex* was then to escort as many of those ships as possible out of the Strait of Gibraltar, protecting them from roving pirate cruisers. Dale hoped that the sight of the frigate, its hull lined with gun ports through which its dozens of guns could be seen, would inspire awe and deter would-be pirates of all stripes from challenging unarmed American vessels.

Dale wrote orders for Lieutenant Sterett aboard the *Enterprise*. The schooner was to accompany the *President* on its mission to deliver official correspondence from President Jefferson to Algiers and Tunis. Dale would attend to diplomatic matters there before heading to his ultimate destination, the regency of Tripoli.

For the fourth ship in the squadron, the commodore planned a special duty. Not fooled by the infamous Rais's assurances, Dale decided that the *Meshuda*'s sailing must be prevented. He ordered Captain Barron of the frigate *Philadelphia* to linger near Gibraltar. "Lay of[f] this port & watch his motions and (act in such manner as your good sense will direct) to take him when he comes out."[4] The American frigate mustn't sail too close, he warned, because the Americans could not be seen to be blockading the British-controlled territory. But if he could, when circumstances permitted, he was to free the seas of Murat Rais's murderous little convoy.

On July 4, Dale set sail for the Barbary Coast, leaving the Tripolitan's yellow flagship just where he found it. The natural protections of Gibraltar's harbor made it the perfect place to observe Rais—the watchful eye of the *Philadelphia* and the threat of her powerful cannons would keep the pirate just where Dale wanted him. In the meantime, the other American ships would do their best to restore peace in Tripoli and salvage relations with the remaining Barbary states.

CHAPTER 7

Skirmish at Sea

I have the honor to inform you, that on the 1 of August, I fell
in with a Tripolitan ship of war, called the Tripoli. An action
immediately commenced within pistol shot. . . .

—Lieutenant Andrew Sterett to Commodore Richard Dale,
August 6, 1801

E
ven if they were not authorized for full-on war, the four
American ships, Jefferson hoped, would win new respect
for the United States of America. The armada's guns were
impressive, and its captains brave, but whether four ships would impress the pirates remained to be seen. Whether the Barbary states
would peacefully back down before a modest show of force that was
not clearly backed by resolve was an even more important question.

When the *President* and *Enterprise* rode the tide into Algiers
harbor on July 9, a delighted Richard O'Brien greeted his fellow
Americans. He then delivered a letter to the dey on Dale's behalf—a
letter designed to offer "the Profound respect which is due to your

Excellency's dignity and character." The note also explained the mission in subtle but clear terms: these ships would "superintend the safety of [American] Commerce."[1] It was lost on no one who saw U.S. Navy vessels that these guardians were armed with many guns, but Dale was careful to make no threats.

Two days later, the two ships weighed anchor and stood out for Tunis, where Commodore Dale would find, in the person of William Eaton, a kindred spirit.

MEN OF LIKE MINDS

The U.S. consul took great satisfaction in seeing Dale's warships enter the harbor. Eaton soon wrote home, "Here commences a new Era in the annals of the United States and Barbary."[2] The two men who met in those days—Consul Eaton and Commodore Dale—quickly agreed that America had to fight—it was the only way. The hostile Barbary nations needed to be confronted. Yet they were restrained by their orders.

Eaton's sense of duty and commitment to his diplomatic mission had been nurtured by a growing belief in the need for American might, but his combative nature was the result of long experience. He had been angry at the dey's tyranny since his arrival in the Mediterranean in early 1799, and his anger had not abated in the following two and a half years.

On arrival in Tunis, he had been summoned to visit the dey in his quarters. Entering the ruler's meandering palace, he had walked through a confusing maze of towers, corridors, and courtyards. Eaton, accompanied that day by consuls O'Brien and Cathcart, as well as several American ship captains, had been led into a small, cavelike room, roughly twelve by eight feet, lit only by the broken light that penetrated the iron grates on the windows. With heads uncovered and feet bare, the men shuffled into the presence of "a huge, shaggy beast," wrote Eaton, "sitting on his rump, upon a low bench, covered with a cushion of embroidered velvet, with his hind legs gathered up."[3]

This was the dey himself, who languidly "reached out his fore paw as if to receive something to eat."

Eaton had been at a loss until a servant barked, "Kiss the Dey's hand!" O'Brien obliged, and the other men followed suit. The gesture seemed to appease the dey because, as Eaton described, "The animal seemed at that moment to be in a harmless mode: he grinned several times; but made very little noise."

Later, an angry Eaton complained to his diary, "Can any man believe that this elevated brute has seven kings of Europe, two republics, and a continent, tributary to him, when his whole naval force is not equal to two lines of battle ships?"[4]

In his years of service since that first introduction, Eaton had found leisure time to observe his new home and tour the ruins at Carthage. He had come to care deeply for the landscape, a terrain utterly foreign to his native Connecticut. "The country on the sea coast of this kingdom is naturally luxuriant and beautiful beyond description," he recorded. "Well might the *Romans consider it a luxury to have a seat here*."[5] He made careful notes about the manner of dress of the Tunisian citizens, noting that they wore "Short jackets, something like those of our seamen, without sleeves, embroidered with spangles of gold, wrought in a variety of figures on the edges and sides." He admired the fine linens and the silk sashes, from which hung swords and long pistols.

The people reminded Eaton of Native Americans, though they seemed much more subdued by their harsh climate and harsh governance. "They are humbled by the double oppression of civil and religious tyranny,"[6] he wrote to his wife back in the United States. To Pickering he remarked that the Tunisian citizens "want that wild magnanimity, that air of independence, which animate those free born sons of our forests."[7]

Increased by the oppression of the Tunisians, Eaton's righteous anger with the dey only grew the longer he served at his post. Even after several years in residence, he was still horrified that the Barbary countries could demand tribute not only from his president (whom the dey called "the Prince of America") but from the rest of the world, too. That European nations would tolerate the pirates' interference in international waters of the Mediterranean was infuriating. In Eaton's mind, this submission to tyrannical force was a blemish on American honor, but his orders were still for peace.

WORDS OF WARNING

Predictably, the Tunisians responded to Dale's greetings with many demands. A few months before, the dey of Algiers had written to the president asking for forty twenty-four-pound guns and forty other pieces. He also wanted ten thousand rifles. Dale could do little but add his promises that the "regalia due to him" was on its way. Fortunately, his words soon proved true with the arrival in Tunis of the *Grand Turk* with its escort, the USS *Essex*, the following day.

Along with Eaton, Dale found his patience growing ever thinner. Dale needed more ships—and the authorization to use them in battle—if he was going to get anywhere. Frustrated by Murat Rais and the leaders of both Algiers and Tunis, Dale wrote to the secretary of the navy on July 19. "I think they must be a damned sett," he railed, "the whole tribe, Algerines Tunisians and Tripolians. [T]here is nothing that will keep there avaricious minds in any degree of order, and prevent, them from committing depredations on our commerce whenever thay May think Proper." Now that he had firsthand knowledge of the situation, he offered his advice for the future: "Keep constantly four or six Frigates in the Mediterranean, without that, there is never any security for our commerce."[8]

With little return for his diplomacy thus far, Dale headed to Tripoli, where he would encounter the most difficult leader of all. Dale hoped to resolve matters with the Tripolitans. If he could not, this time he would be authorized to use force to contain the enemy, giving them incentive to make peace.

The USS *President* and USS *Enterprise* reached Tripoli harbor on July 24, 1801. From beyond the coastal reefs and shoals, the American ships patrolled, seeking to control access to the channels leading to Tripoli's inner harbor.

Though he could not freely walk its streets, Commodore Dale knew that this port city of some thirty thousand citizens was suffering. Tripoli was already partially blockaded by ships from Sweden's Royal Navy, as the belligerent bashaw was at odds with that nation, too. If the bashaw was not hungry, most of his people were without grains and other basic foodstuffs. Dale hoped that his additional blockade, should it become necessary, would hasten the humbling of the bashaw.

On Saturday, July 25, Dale ordered a letter delivered to the town. The letter was long, couched in the best diplomatic terms that Dale could muster. He began by expressing his disappointment at the bashaw's declaration of war against the United States,[9] then followed with fair warning: "I am sorry to Inform Your Excellency—that your Conduct towards the President of the United States, In declaring war against him, has put me under the necessity of Commencing hostilities against your Excellency's Vessels and subjects, where ever I may fall in with them."

But Dale closed his note on a conciliatory word: if the bashaw had any wish to withdraw his declaration of war and make peace, he might send a delegation by boat to the *President*, where Dale would be eager to receive them.

Sunday passed with no response.

On Monday, a boat approached the *President* asking that a messenger carrying the bashaw's response be taken on board. Eager for an answer, Dale granted the request, and the Americans helped the messenger aboard.

The response was given: the bashaw declared, quite simply, that he had not declared war without provocation. No further explanation was offered.

Dale composed another letter, attempting to move the conversation, dispatching it the following day, Tuesday, July 28.

This time silence spoke for the bashaw.

If he had not been certain before, Dale knew the time for diplomatic dodges and niceties had passed, but he wanted to make sure military engagements happened on his own terms. The bashaw's navy was small and diminished by nearly a third, since the *Meshuda* and its sister ship were trapped by the *Philadelphia*. The American navy would be able to take on the Barbary forces in the open sea, but attempting to bombard the harbor was a different matter. Because

Commodore Dale and his captains lacked charts of the unfamiliar harbor, the many reefs and rocks posed a grave danger. Dale decided the wisest course was to blockade the harbor and hope for a chance to engage with enemy ships that ventured in or out.

No ships emerged from the harbor in the wearying weeks that followed. With the unforgiving July sun, the water rations aboard the *President* and *Enterprise* soon ran low. Replenishing supplies meant a trip to the nearest safe harbor, at Malta, several days' sail away. Dale didn't want to lose one of his ships for the week or more needed for the journey, but he had no choice. On July 30, Dale sent the *Enterprise* off, its orders "to take in as much water as you can possibley bring back."[10] Now on its own, the *President* would maintain its watch off the shoals of Tripoli.

BECALMED

Meanwhile, back at Gibraltar, Murat Rais was trapped. Along with almost four hundred of his best men, many of whom were the sons of the first families of Tripoli, he could do little more than listen to the lapping of the waves. He knew that the *Philadelphia* could have only one purpose in staying behind while the rest of the American fleet sailed off. If he made sail, his two ships and their small guns would be overmatched by the long guns of the American ship, and he was not going to give the Americans that satisfaction.

As summer broiled on, Murat Rais and his men faced siegelike conditions. The quarantine had been lifted, and Rais's men could come and go onshore, but they could not obtain provisions. The British merchants on the peninsula, though many had little affection for

Americans (those rebellious former colonists), seemed to revel in this opportunity to refuse the Barbary pirates. With food and water running out, the crew of the smaller Tripolitan ship threatened to mutiny. Murat Rais knew he had to act.

The men in the tops of the American frigate *Philadelphia* might watch from afar, monitoring his ships, ready to intercept them if he set sail. But from such a distance, Rais's men could scarcely be tracked in the bustling harbor. With no guards hovering over them, it was not as if they were prisoners. Could they not flee? That was a question worth pondering. He began to concoct a plan for escape.

BATTLE STATIONS

While her fellow ships blockaded Gibraltar and Tripoli, the USS *Enterprise* made sail for Malta to procure much-needed water. But Lieutenant Andrew Sterett's simple errand was about to be interrupted.

On August 1, the second day out, less than an hour into the morning watch, a lookout spied a ship at the horizon. Suspecting it was part of Bashaw Yusuf's navy, Sterett ordered his men to prepare for battle. Though his orders specified he was "not to chase out of your way particularly," young Lieutenant Sterett was itching for action and ordered his men to sail toward the ship.

Although only twenty-three, Sterett had already proved himself in battle. Two years earlier, as a lieutenant aboard the USS *Constellation*, his role in two victories over French frigates had won him promotion to first lieutenant. The son of a Revolutionary War captain, he took his duty with deadly seriousness: when a member of a *Constellation* gun crew had abandoned his post in the heat of battle,

Sterrett had pursued the seaman and run him through with his sword. Sterrett never doubted he was doing his duty. "You must not think this strange," he explained, "for we would put a man to death for even looking pale on *this* ship."[11] Cowardice aboard a U.S. Navy vessel was a capital crime.

Sterrett was no coward, but he also knew when craftiness should accompany courage.

On this day, the *Enterprise* flew a British flag, as Dale's orders permitted the "use of any colours as a deception." Because Tripoli and Great Britain were at peace, the enemy ship's captain made no move to flee as a ship that appeared to be British approached.

The ships slowed, coming alongside each other at shouting distance. Sterrett hailed the captain, asking the object of his cruise.

Thinking he had no quarrel with this ship, the master of the *Tripoli*, Mahomet Rous, spoke the truth. He had come out "to cruise after Americans." Before Sterrett could reply, the Tripolitan captain complained that he had yet to find any Americans to fight.[12] He should have been more careful about what he wished for.

Acting instantly, Sterrett ordered the British flag lowered as Dale had ordered him to engage in combat only while flying the American flag. As his colors went up the pole, Sterrett in full voice issued the order to fire. The crackle of muskets filled the air.

The Tripolitans, who had at least some of their guns primed, returned scattered fire. The first shots of the war rang out over the water.

A MAN-MADE THUNDERSTORM

Within moments, the American guns produced a deafening roar. Along with the flying cannon balls, streaks of lightning seemed to emerge from the iron cannon muzzles. The crashing sound of solid shot striking the *Tripoli* followed a heartbeat later. At such close range, few shots missed their mark.

Aboard the Tripolitan ship, masts splintered, crashing to the deck. The rigging sagged, and ropes whipped back and forth as the ship rocked; holes appeared in the ship's hull above the waterline.

The first volley over, the American gunners raced to reload: swabbing, ramming, firing again. The well-drilled men hit most of their targets.

Less adept with their guns, the pirates managed to return fire only sporadically. Unaccustomed to relying entirely upon artillery, Admiral Mahomet Rous ordered his men to maneuver their vessel alongside the *Enterprise*. They would board this American adversary and swarm over her sides, knives and pistols in hand. They would fight as they preferred, hand-to-hand, man-to-man. That was the pirate way.

But the small Marine Corps detachment aboard the *Enterprise* was ready. At the order of Marine Lieutenant Enoch Lane, their deadly musket fire repulsed the approaching pirates, dropping many to the decks before they even had a chance to swing their swords.

The *Tripoli* moved off and, seeming to surrender, the Tripolitans lowered their flag. Seeing this signal of capitulation, the men of the *Enterprise* naively assembled on deck and let loose the traditional three cheers as a mark of victory. Within moments, the cheers were drowned out by the sound of gunfire. The pirates, disregarding the rules of war, had hoisted their flag again and were firing on the exposed Americans, who ran to their stations.

The battle quickly resumed and the hellish American fire brought the Tripolitans to surrender a second time—and then a *third*—only to see the enemy's flag twice lower and rise again.

Finally, seething at this treachery, Sterett ordered his gunners to fire until they were sure the *Tripoli* would sink beneath the waves. The cry of "Sink the Villains!" echoed aboard the *Enterprise.* In the long minutes that followed, the pirates' fire grew progressively weaker, but the sustained American cannonade did not cease until Admiral Mahomet Rous called for mercy. The wounded Rous, standing at his ship's gunwale, bowed deeply in genuine supplication and surrender. This time he threw his flag into the sea.

The silence that ensued was broken not by gunfire, but only by the moans of the wounded.

Rous could not be rowed to the *Enterprise* to offer his sword to Sterett, the traditional act conceding victory; the *Tripoli*'s harbor boat was no longer seaworthy, shattered by the cannon fire. Lieutenant Sterett, after receiving assurances as to their safety, dispatched a group of his officers and seamen in the *Enterprise*'s boat. When the Americans boarded the enemy's vessel, they saw a scene of terrible carnage. Thirty men had been killed, another thirty wounded. Bodies lay in pools of blood, as rivulets of red poured through the ship's hatches.

An amazed Sterett found that, in comparison with the slaughter aboard the *Tripoli*, the Americans had sustained no casualties, with no one either killed or injured. He ordered his surgeon to minister to the enemy wounded, as the Tripolitan surgeon was among the dead.

Admiral Rous's ship was in perilous condition. Her sails and rigging had been cut to pieces; one of her three masts teetered precariously before crashing over the side. Solid shot had torn eighteen holes in the hull of the *Tripoli* above the waterline.

Under other circumstances, the *Tripoli* would have been regarded as fairly won and Lieutenant Sterett would have put a prize crew of his own men aboard to sail her to port as the spoils of victory. But Sterett, a stickler for procedure, honored his orders not to take captives.

Instead of commandeering the ship, Sterett's men set about incapacitating it. Cannon, powder, cannonballs, swords, and small arms went into the sea, along with the ship's cables and anchors. After chopping down the ship's remaining masts, the victors raised a spar to which was fixed a tattered sail—just enough to move the boat along. Leaving the defeated *Tripoli* to limp home, the *Enterprise* continued on her way to Malta.

A few days later, on August 6, the crew of the frigate *President* spotted Sterett's battle-scarred victims approaching Tripoli harbor. Maintaining the blockade, Dale stopped the ship and questioned its crew. Anxious to get home, the captain of the *Tripoli* insisted that they were Tunisians headed to Malta who had been attacked by a French ship. Thinking the tale plausible, Commodore Dale lent the captain a compass "& Suffer'd him to proceed on" into Tripoli harbor.[13] The enemy ship had escaped, but only after embarrassing losses.

GOOD NEWS, AT LAST

The bashaw was as humiliated as the Americans were proud. "So strong was the sensations of shame and indignation excited [at Tripoli]," reported the *National Intelligencer* on November 18, 1801, that Bashaw Yusuf "ordered the wounded captain to be mounted on a Jack Ass, and paraded thro' the streets as an object of public scorn."[14] Wearing a necklace of sheep entrails, the admiral was bastinadoed— beaten with five hundred strokes of a switch delivered to the soles of his feet.

The news of Lieutenant Sterett's actions met with the opposite reaction in the halls of the newly completed U.S. Capitol building. With the slow transmission of news across the Atlantic, Americans did not learn what happened off Malta until two months later. But on November 11, 1801, the editors of the *National Intelligencer* declaimed proudly the stunning victory of the USS *Enterprise*. Thrilled by the American triumph, Congress voted to commission a commemorative sword for Sterett and awarded his officers and crewmen an extra month's pay.

To Jefferson, the dramatic vanquishing of the *Tripoli* in the hard-fought three-hour sea battle sounded like political leverage. On December 8, he proudly cited the bravery of Lieutenant Sterett and the men aboard the USS *Enterprise* in his annual presidential message. "After a heavy slaughter of [enemy] men," Jefferson told Congress, the U.S. Navy ship had prevailed "without the loss of a single one on our part."[15]

The encouragement brought by Sterett's victory came none too soon. America had been dealing with the Barbary pirates for years with few results. Appeasement had not worked—poor Cathcart had suffered the results of that tactic. Richard Dale's diplomacy tour had been ineffective—his blockade was letting ships through. The only effective action so far had been the use of focused military power in the face of a threat.

Jefferson was no warmonger. He had attempted to keep the peace despite his instincts. But now he felt justified in calling for America to go to war. It was about time. The Barbary states were already at war with America, and they seemed to understand only one kind of diplomacy—the kind that was accompanied by a cannon.

CHAPTER 8

Patience Wears Thin

I know that nothing will stop the eternal increase of demand
from these pirates but the presence of an armed force.

—President Thomas Jefferson to Secretary of
State James Madison, August 28, 1801

B oosted by the success of Sterett's military action, Jefferson
wanted congressional approval to finally admit there was a
war on. He had no desire to conquer the Barbary states, but
he wanted the newly convened Congress to approve the use of force
so that the navy could launch an effective blockade—a blockade that
could attack and capture ships as needed. With the USS *President*
bound for home and the *Philadelphia* passing the winter in the harbor at Syracuse, in Sicily, a new and different array of frigates and
commanders would need to be deployed, and Jefferson wanted the
authority to fight the pirates properly.

Just a week after Jefferson's message, an ally in Congress introduced a resolution stating "that it is expedient that the President be

authorized by law . . . to protect the commerce of the United States against the Barbary powers."[1] After a brief debate, the House voted in favor and passed the bill on. As January came to a close, Jefferson waited—and hoped—for Senate action.

That waiting for the Senate would turn into two years of waiting for another victory. During those twenty-four months, the Americans would experience little but frustration as blockades failed, a ship ran aground, and a commodore proved incompetent. But the time would not be completely wasted; while America seemed to slumber and the pirates continued to thrive, Jefferson was planning his next move.

FRUSTRATION AND FUTILITY

Jefferson could not know it at the time, but even as he pushed for the House to act, Richard Dale's blockade off the North African coast was producing little but frustration. Dale was forced to abandon Tripoli on September 3. Though his ships had replenished their supply of water thanks to Sterett, the lack of fresh food on board had taken a toll, as more than 150 members of his crew were down with a "kind of Enfluenza."[2]

On his return to Gibraltar, Dale was greeted by the news that Murat Rais and his crew had escaped Gibraltar, though they'd left their ships behind. Tired of remaining in the harbor, Rais's men had threatened a mutiny until their admiral found a way for them to escape their unofficial captivity. Blending in with the crews of ships friendly to the Barbary powers, the men had sneaked past the

Americans and been ferried to Morocco. From there, they were making their way home overland to Tripoli.

With his men safely away from Gibraltar, Rais himself had chosen another route. Blending into the British population in Gibraltar, the man born Peter Lisle talked his way to freedom, and, in September, James Cathcart reported that Rais had been recognized walking the deck of a ship loaded with wine intended for the British government.[3] By the time Dale got word that the high admiral of Tripoli had slipped from his grasp, Murat Rais had long since returned to Tripoli, his bout of shadowboxing with the Americans over. He would fight another day, under better terms.

For Commodore Richard Dale, the news was just one of several disappointments. Not only had Murat Rais escaped his grasp but, in the waning days of October, sickness overcame Dale. "Not feeling easy in my mind," he admitted, he had been confined to his cot.[4] Even more frustrating were his orders to return home. Congress's designated one-year enlistment period meant his crew's term of service expired in a few months. On his sickbed, Dale regretted leaving without humbling the Barbary powers, his only consolation Lieutenant Sterett's success, but he had little choice but to ready his ship to return home.

With the ship's water supply replenished and repairs to the rigging completed, Dale gave orders from his cabin to weigh anchor and take advantage of a fresh westward breeze. The harbor pilot guided the big frigate into Gibraltar harbor's narrow channel but, as the wind in her sails brought her speed to an easy six knots, the *President* suddenly lurched. Her forward momentum slammed to a halt as if the ship had struck a brick wall.

Down in his cabin, Dale reported he felt a "shock so great as almost, to Heave me of[f] my feet."[5]

The big frigate had run aground. She rolled heavily, but as Dale hurried to the quarterdeck, the sturdy ship quickly recovered herself. Dale worried that the *President* might have structural damage and immediately ordered an inspection. The news was surprisingly good: the well-made ship had withstood the impact of striking the sea bottom, and her hull was intact. The officers decided to proceed. They would trust their vessel and continue on their journey.

But almost immediately the ship's sturdiness would again be tested when, after leaving the protected harbor, the USS *President* sailed into a violent gale. On the first day of the storm, buffeted by high winds and seas, the ship made little headway. Then, on the second day, the hold began to fill with water. After changing course to head for the French coast and emerging from the three-day storm, the ship finally made port at Toulon. There, an inspection of the ship's hull found the forward portion of the keel entirely gone, and its extension, the stem, badly damaged. The USS *President* could go nowhere until repairs were completed.

"How long it will take to Heave down & be in readiness again to sail . . . it is out of my power to say," Dale wrote to William Bainbridge from France in mid-December.[6] But he did know that a season of disappointment off the Barbary Coast was to be followed by a winter of repairs. The USS *President* would not reach home until April 14, 1802.

MR. JEFFERSON'S SECRET

While Dale chafed under his enforced rest, Jefferson also appeared to be waiting passively for Congress to act. In reality, he was hatching a clandestine plan. This one was not for the pages of the *National Intelligencer* or the ears of Congress. This plan would not just persuade Barbary states to stop harassing Americans; it would instead change the rulers of those states. So far it was little more than an idea, but that idea had begun to grow.

U.S. consul William Eaton had ventured to write to Secretary of State James Madison, hoping that a strategy that went beyond frigates might meet with sympathetic ears. Learning from Cathcart about the bashaw's bloody path to power, Eaton had a wild proposal. In a dispatch home, Eaton proposed to Madison that the Americans ally themselves with the bashaw's exiled brother.[7]

Bashaw Yusuf of Tripoli had declared war on the United States, but he really had no legal right to lead the country. Hamet Qaramanli, his brother, was the rightful heir to the throne that Yusuf had stolen when he'd murdered his oldest brother. Hamet, banished by his brother, now lived in exile, pining for his wife and four children, whom his brother kept as hostages in Tripoli.

Eaton had met Hamet briefly when Hamet had stopped in Tunis after his banishment. The two men had shared a meal of lamb and vegetables and discussed the best way to deal with the dangerous new bashaw.[8] In the plan they concocted, the American consul had seen a chance both to right Hamet's personal injustices and to solve America's problems once and for all.

Captain Eaton—for this venture he planned to abandon his

consul's garb and don his military uniform—wrote to Madison that he wanted "to attack the usurper by land, while our operations are going on by sea." It would be a military mission, with the goal of revolution in Tripoli, the overthrow of Yusuf, and nothing less than the restoration of Hamet to the throne.

If the idea seemed outlandish at first, Madison and Jefferson realized they had to take Eaton seriously. Eaton had gained intimate knowledge of the Barbary Coast. In his years in Tunis, his skill with languages had enabled him to master several Arabic dialects. He was now well acquainted with the people and their place, and reports had it that he was known to adopt Arab garb, sometimes wearing their robes, and even a scimitar.

Eaton knew the traditions of North Africa as well as any foreigner could. When he reported that "the subjects in general of the reigning Bashaw are very discontented, and ripe for revolt," he spoke from firsthand knowledge. He offered assurances that the United States would not be the only government supporting such an effort—"the Bey of Tunis, though prudence will keep him behind the curtain, I have strong reason to believe, will cheerfully promote the scheme."[9]

For years Consul Eaton had been making a persuasive case for ships in the Mediterranean. He had called for force, and he had been right. Jefferson knew he had to listen to this new idea, but there was no denying that it was a brash departure from all earlier strategies, so he was determined to act prudently and wait for the right moment.

As 1801 ended, Jefferson and Madison conducted business as usual in the nation's capital, publicly looking to get the use of force for a blockade formally authorized. The other plan, the secret plan, was still just an idea, a future option. But far away, on a Mediterranean shore, William Eaton and Hamet, the rightful bashaw, carried on their conversation.

AN ACT OF PROTECTION

On February 6, 1802, President Jefferson got his wish when the Senate approved the use of force. Brandishing his pen, he signed into law "An Act for the protection of the Commerce and Seamen of the United States, against Tripolitan Corsairs."

Though it was less than a war declaration, the legislation spoke without ambiguity. Hereafter, as set forth in the act, "it shall be lawful fully to equip, officer, man, and employ such of the armed vessels of the United States as may be judged requisite by the President of the United States, for protecting effectually the commerce and seamen thereof on the Atlantic ocean, the Mediterranean and adjoining seas." Jefferson could now send as many ships as he needed to North Africa, and they could do whatever it took to keep American ships safe. No longer would Jefferson have to worry that he overstepped his authority in ordering the U.S. Navy to the Mediterranean. Mr. Jefferson's navy could now pursue the Tripolitan pirates as he saw fit.

Although President Jefferson had been shaping a strategy for years, he depended on the opinion of his consuls at the front more than on his own judgment. More than one of his men in the Maghreb had asked for added military might, but Richard O'Brien, writing to Madison in mid-1801, put the case plainly: "I am convinced that Tripoli should have . . . [cannon] Balls without delay. We want sir 3—or 6—or more of our frigates in this sea."[10]

Now that Jefferson was free to act, he honored O'Brien's request, ordering an increase in the size of the American naval force in early 1802. The ship designated as the fleet's flagship was the USS *Chesapeake*. The frigate would join the USS *Philadelphia*, which, along with the USS *Essex,* remained in the Mediterranean convoying merchant ships. Two other frigates would sail from Norfolk that spring, the USS *Constellation* and the USS *Adams.* On returning from the Mediterranean, the master of the sloop *Enterprise*, Lieutenant Sterett, was to turn his ship around again and recross the Atlantic to rejoin the five frigates.

With the new fleet assembling, Jefferson finally had the firepower and the authorization to defend American interests. Intimidating the pirates would be easier than getting involved in their government, and if all went well, there would be no need to secretly plan a coup. Jefferson anticipated a quick and tidy ending to the years of conflict, but he had made one key mistake: he'd appointed the wrong man to lead the new force.

CHAPTER 9

The Doldrums of Summer

The advance period of the season . . . has made it so late, as to render it impossible to appear off Tripoli before January.

—Captain Richard Valentine Morris, October 15, 1802

U p until 1802, the American navy had been suffering setbacks, but these misfortunes were brought about by circumstances, not failures of leadership. Storms, disease, shipwreck, Barbary trickery, and a lack of support at home had kept Dale and his captains from full success. Now, circumstances had changed. The new navy had all of the manpower and authorization necessary to put an end to Barbary tyranny once and for all. Unfortunately, poor leadership would cause a frustrating delay.

Captain Richard Valentine Morris was the president's choice for commander of the new flotilla. A victor in several sea battles with the French in 1798, Richard Morris was a bold young officer who accepted the assignment eagerly. But the thirty-four-year-old captain's marital status had changed since his service in the Caribbean—and it was *Mrs.* Morris who submitted an unusual appeal regarding her husband's terms of deployment. Writing directly to the secretary of the navy, she asked permission to sail with her husband.

The request was not without precedent, but it was rare for a wife to travel on her husband's ship at a time of war. Nevertheless, the secretary immediately granted it, and when Captain Morris came aboard the *Chesapeake* he was accompanied by not only his wife but also their young son. It isn't precisely clear what the sailors thought of the family's presence, but their remarks about Mrs. Morris were not flattering; a midshipman observed that "her person is not beautiful, or even handsome, but she looks very well in a veil."[1] Whatever Mrs. Morris's charms, she had not won over the crew, and her presence seemed indicative of a larger problem: her husband's mind was not on his job.

The secretary of the navy wanted an American show of force off Tripoli as soon as possible, so the six ships sailed not as a convoy but as soon as their individual preparations permitted. Aboard the *Chesapeake,* Morris wanted an easy passage and chose to wait out blustery conditions at Norfolk. After departing at last on April 27, the ship's progress was slowed three days out by the appearance of a crack in the frigate's mainmast. Rot was detected in the great timber, and an inspection revealed defective spars. Making matters worse, poorly stowed cargo meant the ship rolled dramatically, further contributing to a slow and anxious crossing. "I never was at Sea in so uneasy a Ship," reported Morris after finally dropping anchor in Gibraltar on May 25.[2]

Since replacement of the mast and spars was required, the *Chesapeake* could go nowhere until the repairs were completed. But that proved no hardship for Morris and his wife, who soon settled into the busy social life of the British port, dining with the new governor of

Gibraltar and hobnobbing with British royalty. The English officers and their wives welcomed both the commodore and the "Commodoress," as Mrs. Morris came to be known. Meanwhile, disgruntled American sailors found themselves sentenced to remain in port for a period of weeks—which stretched out into months. While their captain feasted with foreign aristocrats, they were stuck swabbing the decks, sewing their sails, and waiting.

A SHOW OF FORCE

As the first of Morris's squadron to cross the Atlantic, the USS *Constellation* had dropped anchor at Gibraltar on April 28, 1802, well before Morris arrived. By Captain Alexander Murray's reckoning, the absence of Commodore Morris put him in charge, and that suited the aging Murray—he was an old salt who'd been a ship's captain since before the War of Independence. He took on provisions and promptly sailed for his post off Tripoli, where a determined blockade was to begin.

After a stop at Algiers—Consul Richard O'Brien came aboard for a briefing—Murray and the *Constellation* sailed east to Tunis and took aboard fresh vegetables and other goods. Captain Murray also unloaded an impressive array of long-promised tribute that the bey found "highly pleasing." This included diamond-studded daggers and gold-inlaid pistols from the finest London makers. Calculated to the penny, the American taxpayers had footed a bill for $27,576.96. But this fresh cache of tribute—it was the cost of doing business in a country with which the United States remained officially at peace— still did not pacify the leader in Tunis, who soon demanded of

Consul Eaton a fully armed warship. Another purchased peace was becoming too expensive.

But Murray did not want to start a new war on his own, and by June 9, he had moved on from Tunis and now patrolled the waters off Tripoli. The American captain thought his ship made a good impression. "It is not amiss," he reported to the secretary of the navy, "to shew these Folks our Ships, now, & Then, they are powerful advocates in our favor."[3] Aside from a trip to replenish the ship's water supply, Captain Murray had little else to report—until the arrival of two corsairs.

They were about to make a mockery of the powerful American frigate.

THE PIRATES' NEW PRIZE

While Morris luxuriated in Gibraltar, on June 17 three corsairs had escaped Murray's blockade of Tripoli. Once in the open sea, the pirates spotted the *Franklin*, an America merchantman bound for the Caribbean, its hold loaded with wine, oil, perfumes, soaps, and hats. When the pirates pointed their cannons at him, the captain of the American ship had little choice but to surrender. The Tripolitans boarded the *Franklin*, put its officers and crew in chains, and sailed for Algiers. There they sold their prize and its cargo before sailing for home with their captives. The story of the *Dauphin*, the *Maria*, and many other ships was being replayed.

Returning to Tripoli, the pirates boldly sailed into port within sight of the *Constellation*. The American ship's size made it difficult for Murray to follow the speedy and maneuverable pirate ships through the shallow coastal waters, so the men aboard the *Constellation* were merely humiliated spectators as the pirates flew the Stars and Stripes upside down in contempt of the American warship. Safely in the harbor, the Tripolitans celebrated with cannon fire in salute of their success.

Once on land, the *Franklin*'s captured captain and his crew were paraded through the streets while Murray and his men made no rescue attempts. Only the intercession of the Algerian dey, Bobba Mustapha, gained the Americans' freedom—but that would be nearly three months later and only after the payment by the United States of $5,000 in ransom.

When Consul William Eaton heard the story of the failure of the *Constellation* to intervene, he wrote to James Madison, "Government may as well send out *quaker meeting-houses* to float in these seas as frigates."[4]

The words were damning. This was no "close and vigorous blockade," as ordered by the secretary of the navy.[5] Although American ships could destroy them in a fight, the elusive pirate boats still interfered with American commerce.

As a Tunisian minister warned William Eaton, "Though a fly in a man's throat will not kill him, it will make him vomit."[6] Even with Captain Murray within sight of Tripoli, the national humiliation of the United States off the Barbary Coast was far from over.

A SECOND CHANCE

A few days after the failure to intervene on behalf of the crew of the *Franklin*, Captain Murray had another chance to confront a corsair.

As the sun rose to fresh breezes and pleasant weather, the *Constellation* sailed easily on July 22, 1802. The ship was a dozen miles northeast of the city of Tripoli when, at nine o'clock, the lookouts sighted ships just west of the town. Though the seas had begun to grow heavy, Murray decided that on this day he would give chase.

Within the hour, the *Constellation* had narrowed the distance enough to distinguish nine gunboats. One of the corsairs fired on the American frigate, but the range was too distant. As the pirates "plyed their Oars, & sails," the *Constellation* kept coming.[7]

At eleven o'clock, Murray returned fire with the pair of guns mounted in the bow. As the battle escalated and the cannons continued to boom, Murray's men took a precautionary depth sounding. Though they were near the shore, the depth of seventy feet seemed safe enough but sharp eyes spied a shallows in the ship's path and warned Murray. Seeing the Tripolitan's "design was to entice us on a reef, which lay between us and them," Murray ordered that the *Constellation* turn away from the wind, avoiding the trap.

Under fire from the *Constellation*, the Tripolitan gunboats scattered, some heading for the rocky cover and inlets ashore. From Murray's ship, now less than two miles away, guns could fire not only on the retreating ships but on threatened Tripolitan troops, now visible on land. Captain Murray estimated they were several thousand in number, including cavalry, which had appeared on the sand hills above the shore.

When the cannons in a nearby Tripolitan fort began to fire at the ships, the shots fell short but still uncomfortably close to the *Constellation*. With the wind shifting dangerously—Murray could not risk being driven into shallow waters—he and his men abandoned the battle and were soon well away.[8] In Murray's judgment, it had been a near thing: "Had they Been 1 mile more to leeward of the reef," he wrote in the ship's journal, "we must inevitably have destroyed them all."[9]

Murray reported on the action to the secretary of the navy, noting that the fight "had a pleasing effect upon our Young Officers, who stood their fire admirably well."[10] Reportedly at least a dozen of the enemy had been killed, among them one of the bashaw's favorite generals. In his mind, the skirmish was ultimately a victory despite his early withdrawal.

Consul Eaton took a dimmer view—he offered direct criticism of Murray and the other U.S. Navy captains and their laughable attempts at a blockade. The incident with the *Franklin* demonstrated their impotence, the Tunis consul wrote to Madison. Two years of U.S. Navy warships in the Mediterranean, Eaton wrote, had produced "nothing . . . but additional enemies and national contempt."[11]

Despite making a good initial show, thus far American naval power had impressed few on the North African coast, American or Barbarian. Only the arrival of Morris and more ships could change that. But would it?

SLOW TO SAIL

When the USS *Adams*, far behind her sister ships, arrived in Gibraltar on July 21, 1802, her captain found Morris's *Chesapeake* still at anchor, though her mast was repaired and she was fully seaworthy. The Morris family was enjoying the high life in the port city and seemed to have no desire to move on to war.

The new arrival carried orders from the secretary of the navy for the lazy commodore. Now three months old, the instructions were clear and specific. Morris was to take his entire naval force to Tripoli. The hope was that "holding out the olive Branch in one hand & displaying in the other the means of offensive operations [will] produce a peaceful disposition toward us in the mind of the Bashaw, and essentially to contribute to our obtaining an advantageous treat with him."[12] The flotilla was to make the case for peace even as it threatened military action.

On August 17, Morris finally left Gibraltar, but still chose not to do as instructed. He made no strong military show off Tripoli, but instead cruised the southern European coast, making stops at friendly ports. At one port he found Captain Murray and the USS *Constellation*, which had left Tripoli in need of both water and repairs. That meant the ineffective American blockade had officially ceased. Far from Tripoli, Morris wrote his first report in several months to the secretary of the navy. Morris would make no effort to reestablish a naval presence in enemy waters—because of the "advanced period of the season," he explained, it would be "impossible to appear off Tripoli before January."[13] The *Chesapeake* would not see the Barbary Coast until February 1803, after spending the winter among allies; more than nine months had passed since it left American shores. The Tripolitan pirates had little to fear that winter.

THE PRESIDENT PONDERS

Back in Washington, President Jefferson had many matters to occupy his mind. Worried at the presence of the French along the

Mississippi, he told Congress in a secret session his plans for negotiating the purchase of New Orleans, and the treaty to acquire the entirety of the Louisiana Territory would be signed that spring. Jefferson and Madison were also engaged in an angry wrestling match with another Virginian, Supreme Court Chief Justice John Marshall, over presidential appointments; the landmark *Marbury v. Madison* case, with its broad ramifications concerning judicial review, would soon be handed down.

Yet despite these distractions, President Jefferson, even an ocean away from Tripoli, was mindful of the lack of aggression in the Mediterranean. Now two commodores had failed him: Dale through no fault of his own, but Morris because of laziness. Morris, it was clear, was a wartime tourist more interested in convoying ships and visiting friendly harbors than sailing at Tripoli. "I have for some time believed that Commodore Morris's conduct would require investigation," Jefferson wrote to Albert Gallatin, his secretary of the treasury, in early 1803.[14] The angry president, well aware that a year had been wasted, indulged in an uncharacteristically sarcastic aside. "His progress from Gibraltar has been astonishing."

Before a change in command could be made, matters got worse.

AN AUDIENCE WITH THE BEY

In the new year, Commodore Richard Valentine Morris at last sailed south to the Barbary Coast. He stopped first at Tunis, arriving on February 22, 1803. For Consul William Eaton, the long-awaited sight of the American flotilla was deeply gratifying. Three imposing frigates in Tunis Bay—the *New York*, *John Adams*, and *Chesapeake*, accompanied by the schooner USS *Enterprise*—made a fine display of cannons and sails.

Eaton's relief at seeing the ships was both patriotic and personal. For years the former army captain had been the most outspoken of the Barbary consuls on the necessity of a show of force in the region. More recently, however, he had also occupied himself on behalf of his country in the quiet pursuit of the plan to depose Bashaw Yusuf at Tripoli. In order to carry it out, America's naval presence off the coast would need to be strong, and now the required ships had appeared.

While waiting for final approval of his plan for regime change, Eaton encouraged Hamet Qaramanli by giving him $2,000, with the promise of more. Although the reigning bashaw offered Hamet a post in the eastern city of Derne, Eaton warned him he should refuse. "Remember that your brother thirsts for your blood," he warned Hamet. "I have learned from a certain source that his project of getting you to Derne was to murder you. He . . . has intercepted some of your letters to your friends in Tripoli."[15] Hamet now waited in exile with his family still held hostage—but Eaton had a larger and more immediate problem right here in Tunis.

He had accumulated debts on behalf of both his government and himself. He now owned two small commercial ships that had made him a prosperous man. But the falling prices of goods and unexpected expenses had meant borrowing money—and his primary creditor was the Tunisian government's chief agent for trade. This debt was a personal embarrassment and, even worse, a serious liability to America's relations with Tunis. Whether out of shame or apathy, Eaton told Morris nothing about his situation. This proved a major mistake.

After a formal written exchange with the bey of Tunis, Commodore Morris, newly arrived in Tunis, was rowed ashore. The country's leader greeted Morris in his palace. After the ceremonial shaking of hands and the ritual drinking of coffee, the two leaders opened up negotiations concerning a Tunisian ship that the *Enterprise* had captured a month earlier. All problems seemed solvable and the men reached an understanding, much to Morris's satisfaction. Then Eaton's debt surfaced, and what had been a personal matter suddenly became an international issue.

As the commodore, his officers, and other American officials stood at the breakwater in the harbor, preparing to return to the fleet, the Tunisian minister suddenly demanded payment of Eaton's debts. Morris, unaware that Eaton could not pay, disregarded the demand and prepared to leave, readying himself to climb aboard a small Tunisian harbor boat hired to row him down the channel to the *Chesapeake*. But the bey's prime minister claimed that Eaton had promised that, on arrival of the American fleet, the debt of $34,000 would be paid—by the Commodore.

The prime minister wanted the money. Now.

Eaton denied making any such promise, but the Tripolitan was insistent and, to Morris's surprise, made clear that Commodore Morris was going nowhere until the debt had been cleared.

The Americans were obliged to return to their nation's consulate onshore.

The next morning, Morris met with the bey, an audience that went on for two hours. As the same ground was revisited again and again, his protests ignored, Consul Eaton lost his patience. He demanded of the bey whether the Tunisian leader had ever been deceived by him.

"You have a good heart," the bey told Eaton, "but a bad head."[16]

Eaton retorted angrily, "[If] my head is bad [t]hen I am surrounded by imposters."

The Tunisian minister, from a culture where to insult an absolute ruler was to flirt with severe punishment or even death, recoiled in amazement. The enraged bey spoke next: "'You are Mad' stuttered the [Bey] in a Phrenzy, at the same time curling his Whiskers." Eaton was courting disaster.

Speaking through an interpreter, the angry bey ordered, "I will turn you out of my kingdom."

"I thank you," Eaton replied, refusing to back down. "I long wanted to go away."

Commodore Morris agreed to take Eaton out of the leader's sight, but that would not be for five more days, during which time Morris would be held under house arrest until the debt was at last satisfied. When the U.S. Navy contingent finally returned to its ship, Consul Eaton accompanied them but, unwelcome aboard the furious Morris's *Chesapeake*, Eaton was forced to find a berth on the *Enterprise*.

Even when he tried to do his duty, Commodore Morris had encountered rough waters. Like Bainbridge before him at Algiers, Morris had blundered into a great embarrassment. As he subsequently reported to the secretary of the navy, "I should not have put myself in the power of the Bey of Tunis."[17] With his superiors in Washington growing impatient, his time to prove himself was running short.

Commodore Morris had one more chance, and it was about to blow up—in a very literal sense.

FIRE AT SEA

Due for a refitting, the *Chesapeake* had been ordered back to the United States. But Commodore Morris was to stay in the Mediterranean and transfer to a new flagship, the *New York*. On departing Gibraltar, Morris made his usual leisurely stop in Leghorn, then sailed to Malta, where his wife and children now resided (a second child had been born in a Maltese hospital), before sailing for Tripoli. Not quite eleven months into his service in the Mediterranean station, the commodore now planned to lay eyes—for the first time—on the place he had been assigned to blockade.

As the sun rose on Monday, April 25, 1803, the *New York* sailed easily just off the coast of Sardinia. At eight o'clock, the drums called the sailors to eat and, tin cups in hand, they waited their turns for their morning meal.

A loud *boom!* interrupted breakfast. The sound echoed from belowdecks and, moments later, the warning that sailors dread most was heard: "The magazine is on fire!"[18] The storeroom where the gunpowder was kept was in flames.

With the rising of the sun, a seaman had gone below to stow the signal lanterns that the ship ran at night. When the gunner's mate later went to the storeroom to check that all was in its proper place, he found a still-burning candle that had been overlooked in the cockpit storeroom. He extinguished the tallow, returned to the main deck, and reprimanded the sailor for his carelessness in leaving an open flame so close to the powder magazine. On returning to the cockpit storeroom, the gunner discovered that he, too, had missed something: the candle he extinguished had started a slow, smoldering fire in a stack of sheepskins. When he shifted the skins, a shower of red-hot coals fell into a bucket on the floor below. Its contents—a small amount of high-grade gunpowder—instantly exploded.

When the flames reached powder horns hanging nearby, another blast blew off the bulkhead door of the marine storeroom. Dozens of blank cartridges were the next to explode. With flames spreading after the series of deafening roars, the nearby powder magazine was in grave danger.

The men in or near the ship's cockpit were all badly burned. But two lieutenants on deck, David Porter and Isaac Chauncey, reacted quickly. They descended to the magazine, groping amid the wreckage in the choking smoke. Using wet blankets, they sought to protect the ship's main powder store—every man aboard knew that one spark in the magazine would cause a chain reaction, blowing the wooden ship to smithereens, killing them all.

The sailors formed two lines, passing water hand-to-hand in buckets to douse the flames. An hour and a half later, the exhausted crew—coughing, blackened by smoke—could take the measure of their losses.

The fire was out, but a toll had been taken. According to the *New York*'s log, fourteen men were "so shockingly burnt that their lives are despair'd of."[19] Lieutenants Chauncey and Porter would survive (and later gain fame in the War of 1812), but four men, including the gunner, died of their burns.

Forced to seek repairs, the USS *New York* returned to Malta. Morris's arrival to blockade Tripoli would be delayed yet again.

MORRIS ON PATROL, AT LAST

For a grand total of five weeks, commencing May 22, 1803, Morris did manage to watch over the enemy's harbor. Together with the frigates *John Adams* and *Adams* and the sloop *Enterprise*, the USS *New York* patrolled the outer harbor at Tripoli. There were several skirmishes during that time, including one where the *New York* delivered more damage by friendly fire to the rigging of the *John Adams* than to the pirate ships. Though the great American warships engaged in sporadic fire with a few smaller enemy ships in their weeks off Tripoli, the fleet accomplished little before once again sailing for Malta.

By early July, his family once again aboard, Morris headed for Gibraltar. He was about to be relieved of duty, and the end of the commodore's service was an anticlimax. William Eaton, having returned to Washington in the late spring, had duly reported on Morris's inactivity. By Eaton's count, Morris had been off the coast of Tripoli a total of only nineteen days in the course of his seventeen-month tour of duty. Perhaps motivated partly by his humiliation at Morris's angry response to his debt, Eaton told the Speaker of the House of Representatives, "It is true that during this term . . . [the Commodore] never burnt an ounce of powder; except at a royal salute fired at Gibraltar in celebration of the birth day *of his Britanic Majesty.*"[20]

When Commodore Morris arrived in Málaga, Spain, he found a letter addressed to him from the secretary of the navy. The words were unambiguous: "You will upon receipt of this consider yourself Suspended in the command of the Squadron on the Mediterranean Station."[21] Morris had been relieved of duty.

Given his lackluster performance, he would be required to face a court-martial. The trial lasted for nine days. After due deliberation, the four-man panel determined that "captain Morris did not conduct himself, in his command of the Mediterranean squadron, with the diligence or activity necessary." His bravery was not questioned; his fault, the panel ruled, lay in "his indolence, and want of capacity."[22] He was forthwith dismissed from the U.S. Navy.

By then, however, the command of a still larger and more powerful Mediterranean fleet had been put in more capable hands. Jefferson wanted the United States of America to have the respect of the world; it was a matter of pride—and of financial necessity—that American trading ships be able to ply international waters safely. Yet the late efforts of his navy sent no message of intimidation. Jefferson put it plainly in a letter to a friend. Morris's tour of duty in the Mediterranean had amounted to "two years of sleep."[23]

This was not effective foreign policy. On the contrary, as former Tunisian consul Eaton had reported, "The Minister puffs a whistle in my face, and says; 'We find it is all a puff! We see how you carry on the war with Tripoli.'"[24] Jefferson could only hope that the new commodore could accomplish what Morris hadn't gotten around to attempting.

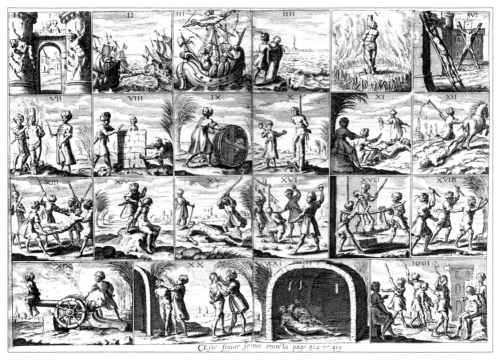

Originally printed in *Histoire de Barbarie et de Ses Corsairs* by Father Pierre Dan (1636), this etching depicts twenty-two different forms of torture by which Barbary masters punished their Christian slaves.

As president, Thomas Jefferson (1743–1826) dared to do what his two predecessors had not: rather than pay for peace and free passage for his ships, he confronted the Barbary powers with military force and, ultimately, earned the world's respect for doing so.

John Adams (1735–1826) and Jefferson were among the first Americans to meet with the Barbary diplomats immediately after the American Revolution, when the friends served as the U.S. ministers to Great Britain and France. Despite face-to-face encounters, the two ambassadors were never quite able to persuade Sidi Haji Abdrahaman and the other Barbary state representatives to stop attacking American ships.

GILBERT STUART, COURTESY NATIONAL GALLERY OF ART

In 1785, James Leander Cathcart (1767–1843) was enslaved by Tunisian pirates and spent more than eleven years imprisoned in Tunis. The language skills and cultural knowledge he acquired in captivity would later prove valuable in his work as a U.S. consul in the Barbary region.

FROM *THE CAPTIVES* BY JAMES LEANDER CATHCART (LA PORTE: HERALD PRINT, 1899), COURTESY NEW YORK PUBLIC LIBRARY

Captain William Bainbridge (1774–1833), though deeply humiliated, had little choice but to agree to the dey of Algiers's demand that, in September 1800, he lower the American flag and take aboard the USS *George Washington* animals, goods, officials, and slaves in order to ferry them to Constantinople.

HOOPER, UNIVERSAL HISTORY ARCHIVE/UIG VIA GETTY IMAGES

As a young lieutenant, Stephen Decatur (1779–1820) was part of the first U.S. Navy fleet to cross into the Mediterranean in 1801. His exploits—most famously the nighttime raid on the captured *Philadelphia*—made him a captain. He would serve honorably in the War of 1812, and, in 1815, prove a hero again in the Second Barbary War.

REMBRANDT PEALE; PHOTOGRAPHY © NEW-YORK HISTORICAL SOCIETY

Commodore Richard Dale (1756–1826) led the first fleet of four U.S. Navy ships to the Mediterranean. A respected leader, he found his options were limited by the terms of engagement specified in his official orders.

R. W. DOBSON, COURTESY NAVY ART COLLECTION, NAVAL HISTORY AND HERITAGE COMMAND

Lieutenant Andrew Sterett (1778–1807) was an early hero of the Barbary Wars, giving the United States its first naval victory in the region.

CHARLES SAINT-MÉMIN, COURTESY NAVY ART COLLECTION, NAVAL HISTORY AND HERITAGE COMMAND

An artist's rendering of Lieutenant Andrew Sterett's leaving the USS *Enterprise* to board the *Tripoli,* after the fourteen-gun enemy ship surrendered on August 1, 1801.

The transfer of command of U.S. Navy forces in the Mediterranean to Captain Edward Preble (1761–1807) marked a turning point in the First Barbary War. Though his tenure expired before a peace treaty was signed, he was responsible for increasing the American presence and launching effective offensive maneuvers in the region.

The long naval career of Captain William Bainbridge was marked by great victories as well as more than one humiliating defeat. One of the U.S. Navy's most memorable setbacks occurred when the USS *Philadelphia*, with Bainbridge as its captain, ran aground in Tripoli Harbor, in 1803. Bainbridge surrendered his ship, and he and the crew were held captive for nineteen months.

In this dramatic rendering from the later nineteenth century, the artist conveys the fearlessness of Stephen Decatur, by then a legendary American warrior.

DENNIS MALONE CARTER, COURTESY NAVY ART COLLECTION, NAVAL HISTORY AND HERITAGE COMMAND

The battle at Tripoli Harbor, on August 3, 1804, with the American frigate USS *Constitution*, captained by Edward Preble, and his squadron preparing to bombard the Tripolitan gunboats arrayed at the mouth of the harbor.

JOHN B. GUERRAZZI; PHOTOGRAPHY © NEW-YORK HISTORICAL SOCIETY

An artist's depiction of Stephen Decatur's fighting for his life—and attempting to avenge his brother James's death—after boarding a Tripolitan gunboat on the day James died.

COURTESY THE MARINERS' MUSEUM, NEWPORT NEWS, VIRGINIA

The USS *Philadelphia* was saved from becoming a pirate ship when, after its shocking loss to the Tripolitans, a brilliant and daring band of sailors, led by Stephen Decatur, set it afire in Tripoli Harbor.

NICOLINO CALYO, COURTESY THE MARINERS' MUSEUM, NEWPORT NEWS, VIRGINIA

The Tripolitan merchant vessel *Mastico* was captured during the war with Tripoli. Converted into a warship and renamed USS *Intrepid*, it played an essential role on February 16, 1804, in the daring and dramatic raid to destroy the captured U.S. frigate *Philadelphia*. Later that year, on September 3, it embarked on one last perilous mission.

PHOTOGRAPHY © NEW-YORK HISTORICAL SOCIETY

A soldier, a diplomat, and, finally, an intrepid general, William Eaton (1764–1811) led one of the most remarkable military assaults in American military history, marching six hundred miles through desert terrain in an effort to restore Bashaw Hamet to his rightful throne in Tripoli.

REMBRANDT PEALE, COLLECTION OF THE MARYLAND STATE ARCHIVES

Hailed as the "Hero of Derne," Presley O'Bannon (1776–1850) led a contingent of seven American Marines and other foot soldiers on a charge of the city's defenses. Despite being greatly outnumbered, the victorious Marines raised the American flag for the first time on foreign soil. In honor of his brave leadership and heroism, O'Bannon was presented with a scimitar, a sword modeled after the Mameluke style, which is still part of the dress uniform of the United States Marine Corps.

COURTESY U.S. NAVAL ACADEMY MUSEUM

In this early-nineteenth-century woodcut, General Eaton and Hamet Qaramanli are pictured at the head of their diverse collection of warriors en route to the defining Battle of Derne. They took the city against great odds in under three hours.

PHOTOGRAPHY © NEW-YORK HISTORICAL SOCIETY

In this twentieth-century rendering, the U.S. Marines assault Derne on April 27, 1805. The events were also immortalized in the opening stanza of the Marines' Hymn: "From the Halls of Montezuma/To the Shores of Tripoli;/We fight our country's battles/In the air, on land, and sea."

CHARLES WATERHOUSE, ART COLLECTION, NATIONAL MUSEUM OF THE MARINE CORPS, TRIANGLE, VIRGINIA

Tobias Lear (1762–1816) served as personal secretary to President George Washington until his death. In 1803, Jefferson appointed him consul general to the Barbary States, where Lear pursued a negotiated end to the Tripoli War, undercutting Eaton's hard-won victory in Derne.

As Jefferson's confidant and secretary of state, James Madison (1751–1836) played a key role in conducting the First Barbary War. As the fourth president of the United States, he would order the U.S. Navy to the Mediterranean once again after the War of 1812. The U.S. Navy finally ended the hostage taking and tribute payments by the Barbary States in 1815.

Decatur's imposing squadron in a show of force in Algiers Harbor brought a close to the Barbary Wars, in June 1815.

CHAPTER 10

The Omens of October

The President is extremely desirous that the United States should have peace and free commercial intercourse with all the states of Barbary . . . but is determined neither to purchase or maintain that peace and intercourse by submitting to treatment dishonorable to our country.

—Commodore Edward Preble, September 13, 1803

Appalled at how poorly Morris had performed, Jefferson took great care in appointing his next commander. He needed a man of both diplomatic tact and courage, a leader who would take initiative and press for his country's best interests. Jefferson's patience with both the pirates and incompetent American leadership had worn thin. It was time for action, so he would appoint a man of action: Edward Preble.

At age forty, Edward Preble had spent more of his years at sea than on land. At sixteen, after announcing to his father that he had hoed his last row of potatoes, he had shipped out on a privateer he spotted in the harbor. He gained a midshipman's warrant in 1779, serving aboard the Massachusetts state navy frigate *Protector* during the Revolution. Although he barely survived a bout of typhoid fever contracted aboard the prison ship *Jersey* after his capture by the Royal Navy, he gained financial success following the war as a captain and owner of a merchant ship. With the establishment of the U.S. Navy, he sought a commission and, in 1798, President John Adams made him a lieutenant. Two years later he gained his captaincy and, as master of the USS *Essex,* spent a full year sailing the frigate across the Pacific Ocean to Jakarta to escort a convoy of merchantmen home.

Preble was not an easygoing captain. When his Barbary Coast orders came through in 1803, Preble supervised the refitting of his ship. While waiting for the repairs to finish, he found time to write elaborate standing orders—107 of them, something of a record. One forbade "blasphemy, profanity, and all species of obscenity." Another instructed officers to learn the names of their men (there were four hundred aboard). But beyond the specifics, one more general message came through clearly: this was no pleasure cruise.

Preble's fair skin had been made ruddy by his years at sea, and he combed his graying hair forward in an unsuccessful effort to conceal his baldness. But his intense blue eyes and his sometimes impatient manner—he suffered from chronic ulcers—conveyed as clearly as his orders did that Preble expected his officers and crew to sail a tight, highly disciplined ship.

From Boston's Long Wharf, Edward Preble readied to sail for the Barbary Coast. With his departure imminent, he wrote to his sweetheart, Mary Deering, expressing his devout hope that "we may again meet and be long happy in each other's society."[1] Unlike Mrs.

Morris, his predecessor's spouse, the woman Preble loved would remain at home, back in Portland, Maine.

In the months to come Preble would demonstrate that he could not be more different from Morris. He would not hesitate to put himself and his just-refitted frigate, the USS *Constitution*, in the line of fire.

When the USS *Constitution* set out on August 12, 1803, she sailed with light but often unfavorable winds, which would make for a calm but long crossing. Preble may have been impatient with the speed, but the uneventful twenty-nine-day sail also meant the captain could become better acquainted with his principal passengers, Colonel and Mrs. Tobias Lear. The colonel was President Jefferson's new appointee to the post of consul general at Algiers following O'Brien's retirement.

Like Preble, Lear grew up on the New England coast, hailing from Portsmouth, New Hampshire. Though Lear bore the honorary title *Colonel*, granted him by George Washington, he could claim no experience as either soldier or sailor. He spent the closing years of the Revolution at Harvard, graduating in 1783, and it was at the recommendation of that college's president that he had been hired for a domestic position at a large Virginia plantation. The job had been the making of the somber, awkward young man with the long nose and lantern jaw.

He was to tutor two grandchildren being raised by an aging Virginia couple and to handle the voluminous correspondence of the man of the house. That tall, broad-shouldered patriarch—known to his family as "The General"—happened to be the former commander-in-chief of the Continental Army, George Washington.

Though of well-established Yankee stock, Lear became a virtual member of the Washington family after his arrival in 1786. He dined with the Washingtons. He had his socks darned and his clothes washed by Mount Vernon's house slaves. When Washington became president in 1789, Lear was charged with making the domestic arrangements in lower Manhattan, the nation's temporary capital, before Martha arrived along with her grandchildren. Lear kept the household accounts, managing the Washingtons' private purse.

President Washington trusted Lear to be his eyes and ears, to report back after "mixing with people in different walks, high and low, of different descriptions and of different political sentiments . . . have afforded you an extensive range for observation and comparison."[2] From 1786 until the general's unexpected death in 1799, Lear remained a trusted member of Washington's circle. It was Lear, standing at Washington's bedside in December, who heard Washington preparing to die. "I am just going," Washington said softly, his throat constricted by the infection that would take his life. Then he offered a last instruction to his trusted secretary regarding his burial. And it was Lear who was said to have burned angry correspondence between Washington and Jefferson.

The whispers about Lear weren't just about the rumored destruction of the letters. There were hints that Lear wasn't quite aboveboard in his dealings with Washington's tenants. And his obvious ambition and close relationships with the most powerful people in the land didn't help dispel the rumors.

If Jefferson felt he owed Lear for the rumored destruction of damning letters, he did not acknowledge it. But during his years as secretary of state, Jefferson had had regular exchanges with Lear, often in person at the president's house. Soon after Washington's death, Jefferson had named Lear to serve as consul in Santo Domingo. On his return from that post, Jefferson turned to him to lead the negotiations on the Barbary Coast.

Just days before the *Constitution* sailed, the secretary of the navy had advised Preble, "Your experience in affairs and your good sense and the tried merits of Mr. Lear all conspire to persuade me that you and he will move in the most perfect harmony."[3] The man of war and the seeker of treaties had become collaborators. It was their task to sort out the mess, militarily and diplomatically. They were to do, in short, whatever it took along the Barbary Coast. They spent the transatlantic voyage planning accordingly.

ON ARRIVAL

A surprise awaited Preble and Lear in Gibraltar Bay. William Bainbridge, whose ship, the USS *Philadelphia*, was anchored in Gibraltar, informed Preble that Tripoli wasn't their only sworn enemy. After confronting a strange ship at sea, Bainbridge had discovered that it carried a kidnapped American crew and orders from the sultan of Morocco to capture American assets. Adding insult to injury, the sultan had obtained Murat Rais's old ship, the *Meshuda*, and returned her to Tripoli. With Morocco joining Algiers and Tripoli in the hostilities, Tunis was the only Barbary state not at war with the Americans, and even that peace looked shaky.

Fortunately for Preble, his squadron was also growing by the day. In addition to the *Constitution* and the *Philadelphia*, three more frigates arrived in port: the *Adams*, the *John Adams*, and the *New York*. Preble also had new options that neither Dale nor Morris had had. Congress had enacted new legislation empowering President

Jefferson to add to the U.S. Navy four warships, smaller and quicker than the older ones, which had been too large to get close to shore and too slow to catch up with the pirates. Construction on the *Vixen*, the *Syren*, the *Argus*, and the *Nautilus* began immediately, and the *Vixen* was ready in time to join Preble's convoy.

Preble saw his challenges escalating, but his orders—direct from the secretary of the navy—gave him leeway to do what he thought right. "We therefore leave you unrestrained in your movements," the secretary had written, "and at liberty to pursue the dictates of your own judgment."[4] He had a freedom Dale had lacked—and the courage that Morris had refused to exercise.

After deliberations with Lear, Preble decided to proceed on two fronts. First, Preble and most of his squadron would present a great show of force at Morocco. He didn't want to expand the war—he could hardly attack Tripoli if his forces were badly divided—but he couldn't afford to ignore this new antagonist, either. He wanted his Moroccan challengers to think he was spoiling for a fight; that might lead to a quick settlement that would then free him up to focus his energies on the threats posed elsewhere in the region. Like President Jefferson, he was convinced that "nothing will keep the [Villains] so quiet as a respectable naval force near them."[5] If a show of power was required, he was there to provide it.

While he took care of Morocco, Preble issued orders to Bainbridge and the *Philadelphia* to sail to Tripoli. They were to aid American vessels along the way, and all pirate ships encountered were to be attacked and captured. Then, together with the *Vixen*, the *Philadelphia* was to proceed to Tripoli to blockade that port and to attack the enemy by whatever means.

CRISIS CONTAINED

When the sultan of Morocco finally returned from a journey two weeks later, the full force of the U.S. Navy was on display in Tangier Harbor. Before the sultan's eyes was an intimidating vista of raw naval power—the American guns, numbering well over 150 cannons, could likely pound the city's crumbling stone castle and sink every vessel in the harbor.

Preble had avoided falling into a trap as Bainbridge had done with the USS *George Washington*. From his commanding position looking in on Tangier, he could choose a tactic that was both direct and deferential.

From his position well outside the range of the sultan's cannons, Preble exchanged letters with that ruler. The two men agreed upon a meeting, and two days before the date the sultan sent gifts from shore: ten bulls, twenty sheep, and four dozen fowl arrived for distribution to the U.S. Navy ships. Moroccan troops and horses were paraded on the shore in an impressive show. The sultan himself made his way to the end of the stone breakwater to view the American ships through a telescope mounted on a tripod. Already he was much more deferential than Barbary leaders had been earlier in the face of smaller displays of power.

When the day of reckoning came—October 10—the American ships had for almost a week been kept in readiness for battle; as Preble noted in his diary, "All hands Slept at quarters."[6] As agreed, Preble himself would go ashore, but he would not arrive in the company of a large delegation. Instead, his party would consist of only himself, Consul Tobias Lear, and two midshipmen serving as aides.

At eleven o'clock, the four men prepared to go ashore, but before they did, Preble issued clear instructions. "If the least injury is offered to my person," he ordered those who remained aboard the ships, "immediately attack the batteries, the castle, the city and the troops, regardless of my personal safety."[7]

At one o'clock, the American delegation was summoned to the castle. The walk through the town did not impress Lear, and he noted the "very narrow and dirty streets [and] the wretched appearance of the inhabitants. . . . There appear to be no shops, no trade—nothing to please the eye or amuse the fancy."[8] On reaching the castle, the Americans were ushered through a double file of guards, but Preble found that the sultan sat not on a throne but on the stone steps in a castle courtyard. One of the midshipmen reported his disappointment at the sight. "I had connected with the idea of Emperor of Morocco, something grand," he wrote to his mother back in South Carolina, "but what was my disappointment at seeing a small man, wrapped up in a woolen *heik* or cloak."[9]

Faced with Preble's overwhelming navy, the sultan seemed almost apologetic. He regretted the hostilities, he said through an interpreter. His country was at peace with the United States, and he would honor the treaty his father had made in 1786. He promised to punish Alcady Hashash, the Tangier governor who had ordered the attacks on the American ships. He would see to it that the captains of the pirate vessels paid dearly, too.

Then the sultan listened as Preble "endeavored to impress on his mind the advantages of a free commercial intercourse . . . and that the revenues of the Emperor arising from that source, would be much greater than any thing they could expect if at war with us."[10] It was an

American argument, a case made for free trade. And the sultan, confronted with America's newfound strength, was paying attention.

The following day, the sultan produced a letter for Jefferson. "Know Ye that all the Treaties entered into between the two nations, remain as they were," the sultan wrote.[11] Several more days were required to exchange and translate the documents that made the understanding official, but the pressure was off.

Commodore Edward Preble had achieved a significant victory without firing a shot. Just as remarkable, tribute had neither been paid nor promised. Preble put it simply in writing home to Mary Deering in Maine once he had returned to Gibraltar: "An honorable peace is established."[12] A clear show of force, backed up by a genuine threat, had resulted in harmony between the nations.

Now, the commodore and the consul had to focus their energies on Bashaw Yusuf and the troublesome Tripolitans. Preble had promised Bainbridge that more force would follow him and the *Philadelphia* after the matter of Morocco had been resolved, and he prepared to keep his word. But neither man could know that the commodore had ordered the *Philadelphia* to embark on what would be its last voyage.

CHAPTER 11

The Philadelphia *Disaster*

> After giving up the chase in pursuit of the cruiser, striking on
> the rocks was as unexpected to me as if it had happened in the
> middle of the Mediterranean sea.
>
> **—Captain William Bainbridge, November 12, 1803**[1]

Cruising off Tripoli according to Preble's orders, Captain William Bainbridge met up with no pirate ships for nearly the entire month of October. The few suspicious ships sighted remained out of reach, staying within the protection of the gun batteries that lined the city walls overlooking the harbor.

At nine o'clock on the morning of October 31, some fifteen miles east of Tripoli, a suspicious sail was sighted near the coast, headed for Tripoli. The *Philadelphia* gave chase. As if to taunt the much larger warship, the unidentified vessel hoisted the Tripolitan colors; it was a Barbary ship trying to slip the blockade, and now the race was on.

The *Philadelphia* was soon at full sail. Though well offshore,

Bainbridge aimed to cut off the smaller vessel before she reached port. Increasing speed, the *Philadelphia* gained on the corsair and, as eleven o'clock neared, Bainbridge judged the little ship might be within range. He ordered the firing of the cannon mounted at the front of the ship. Wary of the unfamiliar waters off Tripoli—other American captains had reported uncharted obstacles and unpredictable winds near shore—three sailors took repeated depth soundings. They reported a depth of forty feet and more, roughly twice the draft of the *Philadelphia*. The ship was in no danger.

The American gunners kept a constant fire as they chased the ship. By eleven-thirty, the city grew closer and the fortress walls could be plainly seen. Rather than put his ship at risk of coming within range of the shore guns, Bainbridge reluctantly ordered the helmsman to change course. To his frustration, he had to accept that he could not overtake the Tripolitan pirates, and the *Philadelphia* began a long, slow turn into the wind, away from the city. The chase was over, and the pirates would go unpunished.

ON THE ROCKS

Moments later, the USS *Philadelphia* lurched with the impact. The ship's great frame shuddered as her bow rose a full six feet out of the water. One moment she was coursing through the sea at the land equivalent of roughly ten miles an hour; the next, she was fixed, immobile, a man-made wooden island halted less than two miles from shore.

The *Philadelphia* had run aground.

The captain stood stunned on the bridge. The charts indicated no reefs, and the last sounding had measured a more than sufficient thirty-five feet. But there was no time to wonder. The men aboard the *Philadelphia* needed to act to save their ship stranded so close to the enemy stronghold.

Bainbridge remained calm and deliberate. He soon learned that the ship's bow rested on rocks just twelve feet below the surface. Consulting his officers, Bainbridge determined to try to back the ship into the deeper water off her stern in order to float her free. He ordered the sails laid aback in hopes the press of sail could drive her clear. Three bow anchors were cast into the sea, their lines cut, to lighten the ship. The guns were shifted back. But as the bow began almost perceptibly to rise, a strong wind and rising waves drove the ship further aground.

Even at two miles out, the distress of the great ship was glaringly apparent. Her bow elevated, the vessel now leaned sharply to one side. To the Tripolitans, the *Philadelphia* looked like an easy target for their guns—and for capture. Nine Barbary gunboats were soon spotted making sail from the inner harbor, bound for the stranded ship.

Aboard the *Philadelphia*, the next hours were a blur. The officers concluded that most of the guns should be sunk to lighten the ship; soon, the seamen aboard sent most of the great iron cannons tumbling into the sea. Barrels of water were cast overboard, and any and all heavy articles dumped. As a last resort, the foremast was cut away. But the ship refused to float free.

A few gunners manned the remaining guns, firing as best they could at the attacking gunboats that circled the stern of the American frigate. But the angle of the ship meant that the guns on one side pointed toward the water while those on the other pointed to the sky.

The well-drilled U.S. Navy gunners could do little, and the enemy quickly recognized their advantage. Establishing positions where the Americans were unable to return fire, the enemy gunners aimed high at the masts of the *Philadelphia*, shattering spars and rigging as they attempted to disable the ship and prevent any chance of escape.

By mid-afternoon, Bainbridge and his officers recognized their situation was hopeless. As Bainbridge later put it to Tobias Lear, "a just comparison of our situation, is one man tied to a stake attacked by another with arms."[2] For the third time in his life, the hapless young captain would surrender his ship.

Bainbridge ordered the gunpowder dampened and the ship's pumps clogged with shot. He sent carpenters below with their augers to drill holes in the bottom to make the ship unsailable once she was in Tripolitan hands. Recognizing the extreme damage done to the British fleet when the Americans got hold of their naval codebook ahead of the Battle of Yorktown some twenty-two years before, Bainbridge tore his copies of the American signaling codes into shreds and ordered the sheets set afire and thrown overboard. Pistols, muskets, cutlasses, pikes, and other weapons were tossed into the sea. If he had to hand over his ship to the bashaw, Bainbridge was going to make sure it was as worthless a prize as possible.

At four o'clock, the USS *Philadelphia* struck her colors.

A SECOND HUMILIATION

The unlucky William Bainbridge almost wished he were dead. This was worse even than his humiliation as captain of the USS *George*

Washington. The day after surrendering the *Philadelphia,* he wrote to his wife, "It would have been a merciful dispensation of Providence if my head had been shot off by the enemy, while our vessel lay rolling on the rock."[3]

With the flag lowered to the deck of the *Philadelphia,* the enemy gunboats ceased their fire. Strangely, however, the Tripolitan gunboats didn't surge toward the American ship. The corsairs seemed either to disbelieve their dumb luck or else to fear an ambush if they attempted to board. Finally, in exasperation, Bainbridge dispatched an officer and one of his ship's boats to assure the enemy of his intention to hand over the ship peacefully. Only then, at six o'clock on October 31, did the Tripolitans board the frigate, clambering over the gunwales.

The Americans looked very odd to the pirates. Spooked by stories of exposed skin that blistered in the noonday sun and freezing desert nights, many sailors had put on three or four pairs of trousers and crammed their several shirts with provisions. The well-clad men made inviting targets, and the pirates tore at the layers of clothing, ripped open the sailors' pockets, and stole watches, money, rings, and any object of value. The officers' swords were snatched and their coats removed; these items were quickly donned by the pirates, who paraded around the ship in their new costumes. Bainbridge had to fight off one pirate who wanted a locket strung from his neck that held a miniature portrait of his wife.[4] The *Philadelphia*'s surgeon lost his surgical instruments. No one was safe from harm when the pillaging boarders began to fight among themselves over the Americans' belongings.

Ordered into the gunboats, the captives were forced to row toward land, their captors "standing with drawn sabres over our heads."[5] Some men were thrown from the overcrowded boats into the sea, left to swim for shore—or drown.

When they landed at the base of the bashaw's palace, the captives were marched through the streets to jeers from the elated Tripolitans. They were prodded past the bashaw's elite guards, armed with glittering sabers, muskets, pistols, and tomahawks. Some of the guards spat on the prisoners as they passed.

Once they were in the bashaw's castle, a series of darkened halls and stairs opened onto a richly decorated room with a variegated marble floor, elegant carpets, and walls decorated with elaborate enamel work. The men were arranged in a semicircle around a raised velvet-covered throne, fringed with cloth of gold and jewels. Seated on it was the bashaw himself. He wore a gold-embroidered silk robe and a large white turban decorated with ribbons. From his broad, diamond-studded belt hung two gold pistols and a saber.

His bearing impressed the Americans. A man of about thirty-five years, he was tall, his beard long and dark. He said nothing to his audience of enlisted seamen, but dismissed the prisoners after "he had satiated his pride and curiosity by gazing on us with complacent triumph."[6] He then had the officers paraded before him.

The officers were fed at the bashaw's castle, then taken to what had been the American consulate prior to Consul Cathcart's departure. There they slept on the floor on mats and blankets. At Bainbridge's request, the man Cathcart had left in charge of American affairs, the Danish consul, Nicholas C. Nissen, was summoned. He promised to do what he could to provide basic comforts and, the following day, he returned with mattresses, blankets, and baskets of fruit. In the months to come, he would be the conduit for money and goods sent to the prisoners.

The officers had the run of the abandoned house and received adequate food, but the members of the crew faced real hardships. Many had arrived dripping wet and gratefully accepted the dry clothing other slaves brought in exchange for their waterlogged uniforms, not suspecting they were never to see their uniforms again. That first night the crewmen were fed nothing and slept in an outdoor courtyard.

The following morning, the men of the *Philadelphia* were questioned by High Admiral Murat Rais, the renegade Scotsman who had commanded the *Meshuda*. Peter Lisle ridiculed Bainbridge. "Who with a frigate of forty-four guns, and three hundred men, would strike his colours to solitary gun-boats, must surely be . . . a coward, or traitor."[7] Finally, the crew was fed coarse bread and confined to a dark and dreary prison, a single large room with too little floor space for all the men to stretch out. Many were obliged to sit or even stand all night, with nothing but tattered sailcloth for covers.

Many were put to work on the city walls. Teams of forty to fifty men transported great stones, ranging from two to four tons, some sixteen feet in length, loaded on crude carts with wheels ten feet in diameter. Like yoked oxen, the men were forced to pull the awkward vehicles, guarded by soldiers with muskets and whips. "We worked bare-headed and bare-footed," reported ship's carpenter Elijah Shaw. "Our necks were burnt to a perfect blister." They were frequently whipped and "the famished condition of our bodies" spoke for the quality of the food.[8]

The officers, on the other hand, were spared such labor. From the terrace at the top of the house where they were quartered, they enjoyed a broad vista of the town, the bashaw's palace, the harbor, and the Mediterranean beyond. On arrival they also took in the melancholy sight of the *Philadelphia*, angled and astride the reef where she'd run aground. On their first day of incarceration, harbor boats shuttled back and forth, returning with plunder from the American ship. Trunks of clothes and other salvaged goods were offered to the captives but at such exorbitant prices that few of the officers could afford to buy back their own belongings.

Afforded pen and paper at the consulate, Captain Bainbridge wrote of the events, not only to his wife but also in a formal letter for dispatch to the secretary of the navy. "Misfortune necessitates me to make a communication, the most distressing of my life," he lamented. "It is with the deepest regret that I inform you of the loss of the United States Frigate *Philadelphia*."[9]

Bainbridge regarded the ship as beyond salvage, subject now to rot and ruin in the waves of the sea. Yet had he been atop the consulate a few hours later, he might have seen one of his fellow prisoners, the carpenter's mate, together with a crew of fifty men, being taken aboard the *Philadelphia*, supervised by their armed jailers. The pirates sensed that a storm was brewing and hoped that, with the wind rising, the morning would bring a storm surge that would lift the *Philadelphia* off the reef. If that happened, the carpenter was to supervise rapid repairs, and the men were to sail her in.

The pirates had read the weather correctly. A violent gale powered by westerly winds raised the *Philadelphia*. The once-stranded ship, lifted off the reef by the rising tide, floated free. Despite the holes drilled in her hull by her carpenters at Bainbridge's orders—or perhaps because of the repairs her men were forced to make by their captors—the sturdy USS *Philadelphia* remained seaworthy.

Bainbridge had bungled again. Had he held on a few hours longer, he might have been able to sail his ship off the reef. Instead, he had once again been part of an unnecessary surrender. Now in the full possession of the Tripolitans, the *Philadelphia* had become a prize of which the bashaw could be well and truly proud. The second prong of Preble's strategy—the attack on Tripoli—had gone terribly wrong.

CHAPTER 12

By the Cover of Darkness

To strike [our flag] to any foe was mortifying, but to yield
to an uncivilized, barbarous enemy, who were objects of contempt was humiliating.

—Captain William Bainbridge, USS *Philadelphia*

Commodore Preble knew nothing of the USS *Philadelphia*'s
fate when, in mid-November, he delivered Tobias Lear,
along with Lear's wife and their baggage, to the consul general's new post at Algiers.

On going ashore, Preble found the city a welcoming place. Richard O'Brien was still in residence, and would remain so until spring
to ease Colonel Lear's adjustment to his new situation. Though the
dey was absent at his country seat, O'Brien gave the new arrivals
the tour.

In Algiers, Preble viewed the ruler's orchards, stables, granaries,
and dockyards. The visitors took a turn through the palace gardens,
which Preble thought so well tended that they had "the effect of

enchantment." It was a most agreeable day, he wrote Mary back in Maine. He concluded that Algiers was "an enviable situation." Being a cautious man, he also acknowledged that "the caprice of the tyrant who governs makes it a dangerous residence."[1]

The next day the USS *Constitution* weighed anchor. Ready to resume the rigors of navy life, preparing to tend once again to his assigned task, Preble ordered the ship's course set for Tripoli to join Bainbridge.

The USS *Constitution* was nearing the Sardinian coast when, on November 24, a midsize ship flying the Union Jack was sighted. Once within hailing range, the foreign frigate identified herself as the HMS *Amazon*. Its British captain gave Preble the distressing news of the loss of the *Philadelphia*.

The commodore pushed the passing pleasures of his day in Algiers from his mind. All in a moment, the successful settlement at Morocco seemed long ago and far away. In its place loomed the knowledge that his hope to subdue Tripoli by spring had ground to a halt on that sandbar.

It pained him that Bainbridge and the 306 men in his command were captives. Preble knew, even in the absence of fresh orders from America, which could not arrive for months, that the freedom of the men aboard the *Philadelphia* must be obtained. Having nearly died during his incarceration aboard the British prison ship *Jersey*, he understood the terrors and trials of imprisonment. And he knew full well these events put the honor of the United States very much at stake.

Then the news got worse. Making straight for Malta, Preble found letters awaiting him from Captain Bainbridge. Not only had the *Philadelphia* been lost to the U.S. Navy but now it was a free-floating Tripolitan warship whose guns could be turned on the Americans. Even as Preble read the dispatches, the mighty frigate was being refitted under the watchful eye of the bashaw. Divers had recovered much of the weaponry that had been thrown overboard onto the shallow reef. Armed with her rescued weapons, the *Philadelphia* was the most powerful ship by far in any of the Barbary fleets.

The commodore promptly wrote to Washington, asking Congress for more frigates. Just a few weeks before, he held a winning hand when his four-of-a-kind frigates awed the sultan of Morocco. Since then three of them—the USS *New York*, USS *Adams*, and the USS *John Adams*—had sailed home for the States, part of the annual ebb and flow of men and ships. Confident in America's powerlessness, the Tripolitan leader would surely demand a king's ransom for the U.S. Navy mariners.

"This affair distresses me beyond description," he confided in the secretary of the navy. Preble also admitted new worries about the solo *Constitution*—"should any accident happen to this ship," he fretted, "the consequences may be dreadful to our commerce in these Seas." With his reduced fleet, he could no longer play the enforcer. At best, he could harass.

While the odds had shifted, Preble could not permit his adversaries to gain the upper hand. He recognized that the *Philadelphia* was the key piece—she must be removed from the game. Two young officers in Preble's command, the dashing young Philadelphian Lieutenant Stephen Decatur and his friend Lieutenant Charles Stewart, had already volunteered to sail into Tripoli and set her afire. But Preble told them that such a mission "was too hazardous to be effected in that way."[2] Left unspoken was that he could hardly afford to lose another ship if they were captured.

Preble did promise the eager Decatur that he might lead the mission once they had a plan. And the more Preble thought about it, the more he realized that any plan would be dangerous—but it was worth the risk. Writing to the secretary of the navy, he promised bluntly, "I shall hazard much to destroy her." He acknowledged that it might mean a loss of life. He didn't yet know how his small armada would do the job—but his mind was made up.

"It must be done," he wrote.[3]

But first they had to prepare a plan.

THE CAPTURE

On December 23, 1803, roughly two months after Bainbridge's capture, Preble's *Constitution* and the *Enterprise* sailed in tandem. The two ships made a fine team, with the *Enterprise* sailing along the Barbary Coast exchanging signals with the *Constitution*, which remained in deeper waters.

Preble was determined to maintain the Tripoli blockade even as he mourned the loss of the *Philadelphia*, but the rigors of winter weather had made keeping up the blockade difficult. During a two-week stormy span, the Americans harbored at the Sicilian port of Syracuse, a break that permitted the installation of new rigging on the *Enterprise* and new sails on the *Constitution*. During that time, the pirates at Tripoli had been free to come and go, but now the Americans were back and ready to fight.

At half past eight on the morning of December 23, nine miles east of Tripoli, the lookout at the masthead of the *Constitution* hailed the men on deck. He had spied two masts on the horizon. Preble signaled the *Enterprise* to pursue the ship they spotted. The *Constitution* would follow.

Young Stephen Decatur commanded the schooner *Enterprise*. Like many of his fellow sailors, he found parading the fleet and blockading ports to be dull work. After all, when a blockade worked properly, nothing happened because ships stayed in port. By nature, he favored more adventure. In his first two tours of duty in the Mediterranean, he had confronted no enemy in battle, and the ineffectiveness of Commodore Morris's time left Decatur itching for the chance to show his mettle. He had hopes for his chances under the determined Preble.

Now in pursuit of the unidentified ship, the *Enterprise* sailed beneath the Union Jack, hoping to keep her American identity a secret. Within the hour, the crew of Decatur's ship saw that their target flew Tripolitan colors. A shift in the wind permitted the *Enterprise* to gain on the boat, which was suddenly dead in the water. By ten o'clock, the Tripolitan captain, thinking he had nothing to fear from the Royal Navy, stood on deck with some twenty of his men, waiting to greet the approaching ship.

When the two American ships abruptly lowered the Union Jack and raised the Stars and Stripes, there was a flurry of confused activity aboard the Tripolitan vessel. However, as his ship was outgunned by the *Enterprise*, more than twice its size, the master of the little trader had no choice but to submit.

A U.S. Navy officer sent aboard the Tripolitan ship was told, through a translator, that the master was a Turk, his destination Constantinople. According to the captain, the vessel, called the *Mastico*, was only a small trading vessel of Ottoman registry, sailing the coast and making stops in Tripoli and Benghazi. The crew of eleven Greeks and Turks was in keeping with his claim. But the assortment of passengers seemed odd to the Americans. In addition to forty-two African slaves, there were two Tripolitan officers leading ten soldiers. The ship also had two cannons mounted on its deck and, doubly odd for a merchant, two more stowed below, along with a cache of muskets and pistols.

The *Mastico* carried no passport in English, and none of the Americans could read her papers, which were written in Arabic and Turkish. But one of the *Constitution*'s medical officers spotted a hole in the captain's story: A few weeks before, Preble had hired Dr. Pietro Francisco Corcillo to be his surgeon's mate, and Corcillo brought more than medical knowledge to the commodore's fleet. Having been the bashaw's personal physician, he knew Tripoli and its people well. When he got a look at the crew aboard the trader, Corcillo recognized its captain and its officers. This was no innocent trader, he told Preble. This ship had taken part in the capture of the *Philadelphia*.[4]

A thorough search of the small ship—it didn't take long, as the vessel was just sixty feet long, twelve wide—proved him right. An American sailor found a sword hidden aboard the *Mastico*, one that belonged to a lieutenant on the *Philadelphia*. It was proof enough to Preble that her men had been among those who plundered the American frigate.

That made the *Mastico* a prize of war, and Preble ordered a crew to go aboard the vessel. They were to sail her to Syracuse where, in February, an admiralty court would condemn the ship, and officially award her to the United States.

By then, however, she had already been given a new name, a new master, and orders to return to Tripoli harbor.

A SPY WITHIN

Preble had been busily gathering intelligence on the workings of Tripoli, but the best information came from William Bainbridge. Under house arrest in Tripoli, Bainbridge could see with his own eyes— and a spyglass provided by Consul Nissen—what happened in the harbor. He also had a means of communicating with the Americans; the bashaw permitted him to send letters, believing that a captive was his own best advocate for securing ransom payments. But because his captors read his letters before sending them, Bainbridge couldn't simply report on the results of his reconnaissance. At least not in the usual way.

Determined to be of service even during his imprisonment, Bainbridge found clandestine means by which to impart information that might be of military use. At first, he employed a cypher, coding his communications. When the bashaw started to suspect the code, Bainbridge resorted to "sympathetic ink," a dilute mix of lime or lemon juice. Using that method, invisible messages written between visible lines on a page emerged as a readable brown when held to a flame. Writing in letters and in books borrowed from the ever-helpful Consul Nissen, William Bainbridge helped Preble lay the groundwork for a secret scheme.[5]

Since his capture, Bainbridge had reported on the business of the harbor, including the coming and going of the cruisers. He listed the ships launched and in the works. He counted the guns in the "Marine force of this Regency (as near as I can learn)."[6] Most valuable of all, he kept his commanding officer informed of the bashaw's plans regarding the *Philadelphia*.

By early December, the ship's cannons had been restored to her decks. She remained moored in the harbor, where her presence was a painful reminder to Bainbridge of that awful October day. But her presence also got him thinking.

His notion, he wrote to Preble on December 5, was to destroy her using powder and shot. Bainbridge thought the job might be done by a "Merchant Vessel . . . [sent] into the Harbour, with the men secreted and steering directly on board the Frigate." The mission faced little danger from Tripolitan artillery, as many of the gunboats in the harbor had been hauled up onto the beach for the winter and, as far as he could tell, only four shore guns pointed at the *Philadelphia*. He was certain the Tripolitans could be taken completely by surprise.

The captain offered his plan humbly. After all, he was the one whose honor was at stake in the *Philadelphia*'s capture, not Preble. "I beg that you not consider me too officious," he wrote to Preble, "in giving my ideas on a conjectural practicability."

When he read Bainbridge's letter, Preble realized that solving the *Philadelphia* problem might not be a suicide mission after all. If he put together his best thinking, along with Decatur's daring and Bainbridge's reconnaissance, there just might be a solution. Perhaps Preble already had on hand the right ingredients: a mix of luck—he already had a "Merchant Vessel," the *Mastico*—and pluck of the sort that the eager Lieutenant Decatur seemed to possess in abundance.

THE HAMET OPTION

Preble was also developing a larger secret strategy. With Jefferson's and Madison's authorization, Consul Eaton and others had continued talking to Sidi Hamet Qaramanli, brother of Yusuf. He still wanted his rightful place on the throne as bashaw of Tripoli, but to get it he needed American help. When letters from Hamet's agents reached Preble, he arranged to meet the men in Malta.

Hamet had traveled to Alexandria, Egypt, they told Preble, and was still very much in exile. But he had a plan, too, and he also had followers. Hamet would assemble a large army of Arabs. If the Americans could help underwrite the venture and provide some naval support, this force might march overland from Egypt to Derne, a provincial capital in eastern Tripoli. With the help of American firepower from the sea, Hamet and Eaton believed, Tripoli could be taken back.

Hamet also had a promise for the Americans, one that Preble knew would please his superiors. If the Americans aided him with money and military equipment in his quest, Hamet, once restored to his rightful place as bashaw, would release all Christian slaves and captives, including the 307 men who had been aboard the *Philadelphia*. He would also agree to a permanent peace with the United States. Furthermore, he would allow the U.S. Navy to make Tripoli its permanent base and to garrison the main fort.

Though he could make no commitment without approval from Washington, Preble applauded the plan—and he immediately wrote to the secretary of the navy saying so. "Though destitute of Money, Powder, [and] Field Artillery . . . he thinks our assistance by sea would put him in possession of Tripoly; and I am very certain that it would in less than two Months."[7] He encouraged Hamet's representatives, telling them something of his thinking about an assault on Tripoli once his squadron regained the ships and firepower required.

While the two sides left their meetings with optimism about what would be done in the spring and summer, Preble's concerns were more immediate. He had told Hamet's agents nothing of the plan for the *Philadelphia.* Even a hint of that plan, if it was to be overheard in the wrong quarters, could result in a disastrous failure and many lives lost.

During Preble's January 1804 meetings in Malta, he had another conversation. The Tripolitan ambassador presented him with the bashaw's demand: $100,000 for the prisoners. There was talk of exchanging the *Philadelphia* for a schooner—the Tripolitans admitted they didn't have the skilled sailors to sail the big frigate, despite the presence of High Admiral Murat Rais, the renegade Scotsman. But Preble was in no hurry to make a deal. For one thing, he lacked the required funds; for another, he hoped the ransom would not be necessary.

A DANGEROUS MISSION

The orders made the operation sound simple. "Enter the Harbor in the night," Preble instructed. "Board the Frigate Philadelphia, burn her and make your retreat good."[8]

The recipient of those orders, Lieutenant Stephen Decatur Jr., intended to execute them to the letter, but Mother Nature refused to cooperate. As his little two-ship fleet neared Tripoli harbor on February 7, a big blow from the north drove both U.S. Navy ships many miles east of their destination. Only after the three-day gale finally quieted did a five-day sail bring Decatur's little *Intrepid*, along with the USS *Syren*, back within striking distance of Tripoli harbor.

Crowded conditions prevailed aboard the *Intrepid*. She was the former *Mastico,* rechristened and reconfigured as a warship. Designed for a crew of two dozen, the little ship was now manned by seventy-five men. With berths for fewer than a third of those aboard, Decatur shared his small cabin with three other officers and the ship's surgeon while many men bedded down among the casks in the rat-infested hold. Spoiled food, heavy seas, and the fear that their little ship might founder did nothing for morale. But at last, late in the morning on February 16, the *Intrepid* was almost at its destination.

The plan called for the *Intrepid* to run ahead, as it had been re-rigged with short masts and triangular sails, mimicking the look of local ships; its appearance should raise no alarms. The USS *Syren* would trail five miles behind. The planners of the mission—Preble and Decatur (with guidance from Bainbridge)—had ordered that the look of the military brig be altered, too, so the *Syren* had a fresh coat of paint. Her topgallant masts had been removed and her gun ports closed.

As dark approached, the *Intrepid* was to anchor at the mouth of the harbor, east of the town. Then, after the arrival of the *Syren*, the *Intrepid* and the boats from the *Syren* would make for the *Philadelphia* under the cover of night. The lieutenants and midshipmen would then lead teams of sailors aboard the frigate to set her afire. They would destroy the ship, boosting American morale and snatching the advantage from their enemies. It would be a master stroke—if it worked.

Almost immediately, the plan went awry. Decatur realized that the easy sail into Tripoli was too easy: the *Intrepid*, normally a slow sailer, was making good speed and ran the risk of arriving in daylight. Not daring to shorten the sails—a wary sentinel might be suspicious of a merchant slowing his progress—Decatur ordered his men to toss overboard a drag line rigged with ladders, spars, buckets, and lumber in hopes that the resistance of all of the debris would slow the ship down.

After a scramble of activity to get the drag line overboard, there were a few tense minutes of waiting. Then the sailors breathed a sigh of relief as the ship slowed while still appearing to be sailing full speed ahead. Their plan had worked, and they could count on the darkness to help avoid discovery.

Decatur ordered most of his crew to remain below. Just six men at a time could walk the deck, and those who did wore the uniform of Maltese merchant sailors, with showy gold braid. The British flag they flew also seemed to fool those onshore. As they came within sight of the English fort at Tripoli, the English colors that waved over the *Intrepid* were answered by the raising of the Union Jack at the British consulate.

For Decatur, this slow sail into Tripoli was bittersweet. He had asked to head this dangerous expedition and desperately wanted to prove his bravery in battle. His reward for success, he hoped, would be a captaincy in the small U.S. Navy, where only a few gained such a promotion. But his assignment was to destroy a ship built with money raised by the citizens of and handmade by the shipwrights of his home city, for which the frigate was named. And her first captain had been his own father, Stephen Decatur Sr.

At dusk, the wind dropped. As the *Intrepid* negotiated the narrows at the harbor entrance at seven o'clock, Decatur could see that the *Syren* had fallen well behind in the diminishing breeze, despite the *Intrepid*'s intentional slowdown. It was a moment for naval calculus: the plan called for an attack at ten o'clock, and it would take much of the time remaining for Decatur to work his ship over to the

Philadelphia. The *Syren* was well back, and it would not be able to make up the distance in time.

For Decatur, failure was not an option. He remembered Preble's orders: "I rely with confidence on your Intrepedity & Enterprize."[9] Decatur saw his choice as between aborting the mission and taking the *Intrepid* in alone.

In the twilight, he had little time to decide. Emboldened by the frustrations of serving under Morris, proud of the trust Preble put in him, Decatur made the call. He told his men they would sail on, despite the absence of the *Syren.*

One of his midshipmen recorded Decatur's quiet words: "The fewer the number the greater the honor."[10]

As darkness fell, the light of a crescent moon revealed the *Philadelphia* in silhouette. She was a heartrending sight to Decatur and his men. Her foremast remained a stump, and her upper yards were laid out on the deck. Stripped of sails, she could go nowhere under her own power. Yet her sheer scale seemed awesome in a harbor where little local boats skimmed the waves. To see the frigate's guns remounted and to imagine them manned by Tripoli pirates? That was too horrible even to contemplate.

The *Intrepid* made her way slowly down the channel, an almost imperceptible wind puffing her sails. The castle and shore fortifications seemed to grow taller as the crew covered the distance. Decatur's little ship was dwarfed as it floated closer to the white walls of the city—and the gun batteries on her ramparts. Any lookout from the city could see them, but he would have no reason to be alarmed by the little ship's appearance.

As the ten o'clock hour approached, the *Intrepid* came within hailing distance of the *Philadelphia*. Decatur's seventy-man crew, obeying his order of wordless silence, heard the exchange.

A Tripolitan spoke from the tall frigate. In a foreign tongue, he ordered the smaller vessel to keep away.

Though he stood by the helm, Decatur remained silent. In his stead, Salvador Catalano answered. A Sicilian hired by Preble for his knowledge of Barbary harbors, Catalano was fluent in the common tongue of sailors in the southern Mediterranean, a mix of Berber, Arabic, Italian, Spanish, Portuguese, and Maltese.

Catalano called back that his merchant vessel had been stripped of its anchors during the violent storm the preceding week; they sought only a safe place to tether their little ship for the night. He explained that they didn't want to risk fouling the lines of other ships in the harbor and, in the morning, would secure new anchors ashore.

Another voice from above asked the name of the ship observed offshore in the direction from which the *Intrepid* had come. Catalano offered a well-rehearsed reply, one he knew the men aboard the *Philadelphia* wanted to hear. He told his inquisitor the ship they spied was the *Transfer*. That vessel was a former British warship, recently purchased in Malta by the bashaw, and much awaited in Tripoli to reinforce his navy.

Catalano's answers satisfied the men aboard the *Philadelphia*, and the two ships—the little *Intrepid* and the looming frigate— dispatched boats carrying lines to fasten them to each other. With the cables bound fast, the ships were soon being drawn together.

As the *Intrepid* neared, a sharp-eyed Tripolitan spotted something amiss. Perhaps the anchors aboard the *Intrepid* had been seen. Maybe it was the glint of sword worn by one of the dozens of sailors lying in the shadows cast by the bulwarks. Whatever the tell, the game was nearly up.

"Americanos!" came the cry.

Once again Catalano spoke, his manner unruffled. He offered assurances that only Maltese and Englishmen were aboard. With the men aboard the *Intrepid* continuing to haul the hawsers, the ships were soon alongside.

This time, when the shout *"Americanos! Americanos!"* rang out again, the warning came too late. As the ships touched, Stephen Decatur issued a simple order, uttered as he himself leapt for the main chains of the *Philadelphia* to climb the dozen feet to the deck of the taller ship.

The one-word order—*"Board!"* Decatur yelled—initiated a blur of action.

"The effect was truly electric," Surgeon's Mate Lewis Heermann would later write. "Not a man had been seen or heard to breathe a moment before; at the next, the boarders hung on the ship's side like cluster bees; and, in another instant, every man was on board the frigate."[11]

No gunshots echoed. Decatur had decreed that only blades were to be used, because the invaders wanted to attract as little attention as possible to the fight for the *Philadelphia*, which was moored just a few hundred yards from the fortress guns. Of the thirty or so Tripolitans aboard the ship, roughly a dozen ran for a boat and rowed for safety. Of those who fought the boarding party, one midshipman remembered, "[They] were dreadfully alarmed when they found who we were. Poor fellows! About 20 of them were cut to pieces & the rest jumped overboard."[12]

In less than ten minutes, the savage fight was over without having attracted the notice of sentries onshore, and the carefully planned torching of the ship could begin. A team of ten men went below to set fire to the berth deck and forward storeroom. A dozen men went deeper into the ship to the wardroom and steerage, a third squad to the cockpit and storeroom. A fourth team manned the *Intrepid*'s cutter, patrolling the area in the harbor boat used to ferry passengers and goods, while eight men remained aboard the little ketch.

The fire crews carried three-inch-long candles, with wicks that had been immersed in turpentine to enhance their flammability, and each team had a pair of lanterns. With the Tripolitan defenders subdued, combustibles were swiftly handed up from the *Intrepid* and taken below. The disciplined operation proceeded at speed and, in a matter of minutes, the men waited at their stations for Decatur's next command.

Walking the deck from forward to aft, he called his simple order down each hatchway—*Fire!*—and the men, their candles lit from the lanterns, ignited dozens of conflagrations in every part of the ship.

As the men raced to return to the deck, columns of suffocating smoke rose in columns from the hatches. Flames soon followed as the sailors and officers alike leapt back aboard the *Intrepid*. Decatur watched as the last of his men climbed down to the deck of the ketch—only one sailor had been wounded, none killed. Decatur himself would be the last man to step off the deck of the *Philadelphia*— and he did so in dramatic style, leaping into the rigging of the *Intrepid*.

Back aboard their little ship, the crew attempted to escape the harbor but were momentarily trapped. The flames roaring forth from every gun port on the *Philadelphia* threatened the cotton sail fluttering from the foremast of the getaway boat. They used swords to cut the rope connecting the two boats, but the smaller ship still refused

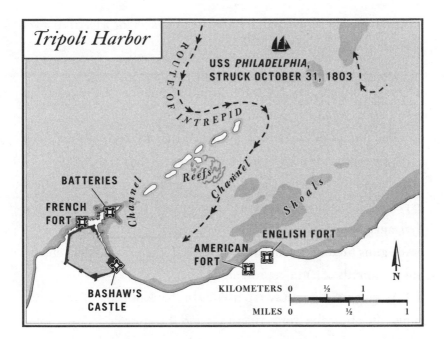

Tripoli Harbor

ROUTE OF INTREPID

USS *PHILADELPHIA*,
STRUCK OCTOBER 31, 1803

BATTERIES

FRENCH
FORT

Channel

Reefs

Channel

Shoals

ENGLISH FORT

AMERICAN
FORT

BASHAW'S
CASTLE

KILOMETERS 0   ½   1

MILES 0   ½   1

N

to sail free. The hungry fire, which seemed to be inhaling every breath of air, drew the *Intrepid* back. Only after Decatur ordered a crew to man a boat to tow the bow around did the sails fill. Men took hold of the great oars, eight to a side, and stroked until they were in open water.

As the *Intrepid* made her retreat, harassing fire from Tripolitan cannons and muskets threatened Decatur's vessel, but the poorly aimed gunfire struck only her upper sails. Much more dangerous than the volleys from shore were the cannons aboard the *Philadelphia*, which discharged as the fire consumed the gun deck. But even the report of the frigate's long guns could not drown out the three hearty cheers issuing from the American sailors as they headed out to sea. By then flames had licked up the mastheads and begun consuming the rigging at the tops. The sight of the columns of flame, topped with what appeared to be fiery capitals, made a terrifying yet magnificent sight in the night sky of Tripoli.

The night of February 16, 1804, would be one that the imprisoned crew of the *Philadelphia* would never forget.

The tumult in the harbor awakened the city and, in the prison yard, the captives heard the screams of women; the harsh, loud voices of men; and the report of the guns in the harbor. The Americans had expected something as they had recognized the *Intrepid* and the *Syren* just out of reach of the harbor the previous afternoon. As the castle guns fired on the departing *Intrepid*, the prison floors shook, but the sounds of battle represented hope.

As sailor William Ray reported, "In the confusion of voices we could often hear the word American, and therefore hoped that some of our countrymen were landing, to liberate us."[13] Their hope for rescue was not realized, they found the next morning, when they learned of the demise of the *Philadelphia*. The once proud ship now lay on the rocks, free of her anchors after her cables burned. She was a smoking hulk, reduced to a long row of ribs barely visible at the waterline. The frigate would never put to sea as a pirate ship.

The burning of the American ship was a victory for the American navy but a blow for the captives. Just the day before the bashaw, anticipating that his terms of a prisoner exchange would be accepted, had sent two barrels of pork and beef to the men in the bagnio. Now, with the burning of the *Philadelphia*, all goodwill evaporated just as quickly as it had appeared. The jail keepers, Ray reported, "like so many fiends from the infernal regions, rushed in among us and began to beat everyone they could see, spitting in our faces, and hissing like the serpents of hell. . . . [E]very boy we met in the streets, would spit on us and pelt us with stones; our tasks doubled, our bread withheld, and every driver exercised cruelties tenfold more rigid and intolerable than before."[14]

Unaware of the suffering of their compatriots, Decatur and his men were well on their way to safety, and a two-day sail brought them within range of Syracuse harbor. The sight of the *Intrepid* and the *Syren* was a great relief to Commodore Preble; he had wondered at the seaworthiness of the little ship a week before when the violent storm had buffeted his ships at anchor. Both ships could have gone down, yet here they were.

Signal flags were quickly hoisted. The USS *Constitution* signaled: *"Business or Enterprize, have you completed, that you were sent on?"*

On the quarterdeck of the frigate, anxious minutes ticked by. Then the answering flags could be read slowly. For Preble, it was most gratifying to read the message: *"Business, I have completed, that I was sent on."*

CHAPTER 13

The Battle of Tripoli

I find hand to hand is not child's play, 'tis kill or be killed.

—Lieutenant Stephen Decatur[1]

More than four months passed before anyone in Washington knew anything of the fate of the USS *Philadelphia*. Since the previous autumn of 1803, mail had accumulated in Malta; letters home from sailors, dispatches from Preble, and consular correspondence remained unsent. Only when Commodore Preble stumbled upon a cache of mail in the charge of a former consul to the bashaw who spoke no English did four great stacks of long-delayed correspondence begin their transatlantic journey in early February.[2]

That meant President Jefferson learned of the grounding of the USS *Philadelphia*—but not of its sacrificial fire—on March 19, 1804. It also meant that, for the third winter in a row, despite Preble's good efforts, only ill tidings reached Washington from the Barbary Coast.

Jefferson's political enemies used the news of the frigate's capture like a club. By the end of March, Alexander Hamilton's *New York Evening Post* termed it "a practical lesson in Jefferson's economy"—if there'd been more ships in the Mediterranean, the argument went, the loss could have been averted.[3] Rather than disagree, Jefferson went to Congress and made the argument that the bad news meant even more firepower was needed. Within a week, he had authorization to spend a million dollars to supplement the fleet with leased gunboats and two new ships. In addition, a bill was introduced to raise customs duties by 2.5 percent to establish a "Mediterranean Fund" to pay for the war. The House unanimously approved the measure and, the same day, the Senate passed it by a vote of 20 to 5.

Orders went out for four more frigates to sail for the Mediterranean. With almost the entire U.S. Navy in or on its way to service off the North African coast, Jefferson intended "to leave no doubt of our compelling the existing Enemy to submit to our own terms, and of effectually checking any hostile dispositions that might be entertained towards us by any of the other Barbary Powers."[4] The *President*, *Congress*, *Essex*, and *Constellation* would require time to be refitted and provisioned, so the latest fleet—all veteran ships at this point—would not return to the region until summer, but the full force of the United States Navy had finally been mustered.

Behind the scenes, Secretary of State Madison quietly tried to allay the concerns of the families of the 307 *Philadelphia* men in captivity, offering the "sympathy of the Executive." But he made no promises. The U.S. government wouldn't be offering to buy the freedom of Captain Bainbridge and his men anytime soon because "of the encouragement it might hold out to the other Barbary States, and even to Tripoli, to repeat their aggressions."[5]

Then, like a lightning bolt, the news of Decatur's successful raid electrified Washington. Word of the burning of the *Philadelphia* had already shocked Europe. No less a military man than Lord Nelson called Decatur's exploit "the most bold and daring act of the age."[6] On hearing the news, Jefferson promptly awarded his brave lieutenant a captaincy (though Decatur would not learn of his promotion until September), and Congress voted to award Decatur a ceremonial sword and his men two months' bonus pay. The entire country celebrated. By early June, New Yorkers saw the opening of a silent play, a pantomime entitled *Preparations for the Recapture of the Frigate Philadelphia*.

Stephen Decatur and his seventy-five-man crew had transformed a humiliation into an act of heroism. For Jefferson, this shift in tides also had a practical meaning. As one Barbary consul told James Madison, "The burning of the *Philadelphia*, under the Bashaw's forts . . . is the only occurrence, which has forced them to view the *American character* with proper respect."[7] This was progress, a long-awaited sign that American forces could make a significant difference in the region.

IF NOT PEACE, THEN BOMBARDMENT

Meanwhile, on the other side of the Atlantic, Commodore Preble decided he would give peace one more chance—and he hoped to gain freedom for the men of the *Philadelphia*. An array of American ships bore up on Tripoli harbor on a June day in 1804. Captain Preble stationed the USS *Argus* and the USS *Enterprise* as lookouts to the west. He sent the USS *Vixen* to the east, along with his newest ship, the *Scourge*, recently captured from the Tripolitan navy.

Flying a white flag of truce, he ordered his flagship, the USS *Constitution*, to set sail for the city. At noon on June 13, 1804, anchored where the water was a safe depth of twenty-four fathoms, Preble dispatched a barge carrying Richard O'Brien to present American terms of peace to Bashaw Yusuf Qaramanli. Chief Consul Tobias Lear, unable to leave his post in Algiers, had deputized O'Brien to act as his representative.

As the little vessel neared shore, O'Brien could see some of the *Philadelphia*'s officers waving their hats at him. He would have liked nothing better than to secure their freedom before the day was over.

Preble's charge to O'Brien sounded simple: "to endeavor to ransom our unfortunate Countrymen, and if the bashaw should desire it, to establish Peace."[8] Lear had authorized a larger payment, but Preble specified what he thought were reasonable terms. O'Brien was instructed to offer $40,000 in ransom, along with a $10,000 "present" (that is, bribe) for the prime minister and others. A treaty of peace might be entered into, but, Preble told O'Brien, "I cannot pay one cent for Peace."[9] Payment for ransom was a stretch as it was.

The bashaw's representatives kept O'Brien waiting for an hour on the beach. "The Tyrant," as Preble called the Tripolitan ruler, still beside himself at the burning of the *Philadelphia* within sight of his own castle, refused to see O'Brien and rejected the offer relayed to him out of hand. He was insulted by the offer; it was so much less than he had imagined, *and* he suspected the Americans' real motive was espionage. Thinking O'Brien might be gathering intelligence about the city and its armaments, he refused permission for the American consul to enter the town and forbade him to meet with Captain Bainbridge or visit the other prisoners. He did not allow clothing to be sent ashore for the captives, and his men dropped the white flag of truce as soon as O'Brien returned to the *Constitution*.

The conclusion was clear. Once again, as Preble confided to his diary, we "must endeavor to beat & distress his savage highness into a disposition more favourable to our views than what he at present possesses."[10] Persuasion and pacifism had not worked. The Americans would have to speak to the bashaw in a way that would force him to respond reasonably. That, Preble believed, was something a bombardment could certainly do.

WILLIAM EATON, SECRET AGENT

Meanwhile, at home, the news of the *Philadelphia* had been good for William Eaton's pet cause. After his expulsion by the bey of Tunis in early March 1803, Eaton had returned to the United States. On arrival at Boston in May, he visited his wife in the central Massachusetts town of Brimfield; they had been separated by an ocean for four and a half years. By June, however, he was striding the streets of the nation's capital, "urg[ing] the administration to the adoption of more vigorous measures against Tripoli."[11]

More than anything, Eaton wanted to persuade the powers that be to support his plan to replace Bashaw Yusuf on Tripoli's throne with the exiled Hamet Qaramanli. He also wanted to be the leader of the expedition that would land in Alexandria, join Hamet, and march to Derne, as Preble schemed. Eaton was the driving force on the American side, writing to the Speaker of the House of Representatives, detailing his case and meeting with Secretary of State Madison.

In a meeting with the president's cabinet, Eaton thought Jefferson *"civil"* and his attorney general *"grave"* as he "endeavored to enforce conviction . . . of the necessity of meeting the aggressions of Barbary by retaliation."[12] The secretary of war was skeptical, but the secretary of the navy, Robert Smith, was won over. Growing cautiously optimistic, Eaton commissioned a custom scimitar to be fashioned for himself of the finest Spanish steel. He also ordered tents, saddles, and cooking equipment. He wanted to be ready.[13]

Eaton had at least one ally in Preble, but for a time nothing had happened. With the congressional session at an end, Eaton traveled north. He spent much of the summer and fall tending to his hardscrabble New England farm. During the next congressional session, however, he returned to Washington. If at first he again found many of those he met indifferent to him, the news of the loss of the USS *Philadelphia* shifted the balance. Suddenly, there were ears in Washington more attuned to his ideas. On March 30, 1804, eleven days after the shocking news of the frigate's grounding but not her destruction had reached American shores, Eaton was "engaged to take the management of an Enterprize on the coast of Barbary."[14]

The long, sticky summer that followed proved eventful for the young nation. The exploration team led by Meriwether Lewis and William Clark began its journey up the Missouri River. In July, Alexander Hamilton was shot and killed in a duel by Vice President Aaron Burr, and the further conflict in Europe provoked by Napoleon had America's foreign affairs in a state of uncertainty.

As for President Jefferson, he was dealing with his own personal tragedy. His beloved Mary, whom he had nicknamed "Polly" so long ago and whose safety upon the seas had made the matter of Barbary piracy personal, died in childbirth in April. Her father and her husband were both at her deathbed, and she was buried beside her mother on the grounds of Monticello. Jefferson was deeply affected by Polly's passing. "My loss is great indeed," he wrote to a friend in June. "Others may lose of their abundance, but I, of my want, have lost even the half of all I had. . . . The hope with which I had looked forward to the moment when, resigning public cares to younger hands, I was to retire to that domestic comfort from which the last great step is to be taken, is fearfully blighted."[15]

Jefferson was nearing the end of his first term as president and eyeing a second one, but his passion for life and zeal for leadership had been extinguished with Polly's death. Former first lady Abigail Adams, wife of Jefferson's friend and rival John Adams, broke the years-long silence between the two families by sending her deepest condolences. The gesture proved to be the first step in mending the friendship that had been so deeply—and some thought irreconcilably—damaged during the contentious election of 1800.

But world events would not stop for Jefferson's mourning. Eaton's quest moved forward, with Eaton ordered to act as a liaison with Hamet. Madison wrote to the Barbary chief consul Tobias Lear authorizing the plan, though he did so in his usual cautious fashion. "Of the co-operation of the Elder brother of the Bashaw of Tripoli we are . . . willing to avail ourselves."[16] Madison also instructed Lear to make available to Eaton $20,000 to carry out the plan.

There were other changes to the American strategy as well. The time had come for another changing of the guard and, after serving honorably and with distinction, Preble was to return home and Commodore Samuel Barron, who had been with the first fleet as the captain of the *Philadelphia* two years before her fateful wreck, was to take his place. In his orders to the new squadron commander, the secretary of the navy authorized a plan involving the ex-bashaw—one in which, the secretary advised, "you will, it is believed, find Mr Eaton extremely useful to you."[17]

When, after multiple delays, Commodore Barron's squadron sailed from Norfolk on July 5, 1804, one of those aboard his flagship was William Eaton, U.S. Navy agent for the Barbary regencies. Eaton's salary was a modest $1,200 a year and his immediate task was to win Barron's enthusiastic support before he could throw himself into planning the ground offensive.

He knew he was embarking on the adventure of a lifetime, but he had no idea the extent of the warfare into which he was sailing.

A SMALL VICTORY

In the Mediterranean, on August 3, 1804, the long-suppressed tension in the bashaw's harbor broke out into battle.

Commodore Preble had spent much of the previous week dealing with heavy seas off the Tripoli coast where he tried to maintain his blockade. A strong gale brought the month of July to a close, and Preble, with a new assortment of ships at his command, had new worries as well. He knew the schooners accompanying him, the *Vixen* and *Nautilus*, were seaworthy, as were the two brigs *Argus* and *Syren*, which had been blockading the harbor for many weeks. But he couldn't be so sure about the six gunboats and the two mortar boats on loan from Sicily, which was now also at war with the bashaw. Preble had reached an understanding to borrow these boats, along with some men to sail them, but he worried whether the flat-bottomed harbor craft could withstand the weather of the open sea.

Somehow, though, they had, and now he would put them to the test in battle.

With the weather clear at last, Preble surveyed his enemy from the deck of the *Constitution*. Through his spyglass he counted 115 guns mounted on the city's fortifications. These cannons were supplemented by nineteen gunboats and several small corsairs, all sheltered behind the long line of rocks that, like an immense, submerged stone wall, stood between the American armada in the open sea and the protected harbor. The combined firepower of the American and allied ships—132 guns and 2 mortars—was more or less equal to the Tripolitan guns, but the range of most of Preble's short-barreled cannonades was limited. Still, Preble felt confident that he and his men could make "[the bashaw's] old walls rattle about his ears."[18] All he needed was the opportunity.

Then, at noon on August 3, Preble finally saw his chance to engage the enemy. He observed from his station two miles out to sea that enemy gunboats were coming out from behind the stony barrier reef, leaving them exposed in the open water. He ordered the signal hoisted: *Prepare for battle.*

With his entire flotilla within hearing distance of his hailing trumpet, the commodore issued his final orders. The brigs and schooners, with the gunboats in tow, were to sail halfway to the stone barrier. From there the gunboats would head for the shore while the four larger ships remained in deeper waters. The bombing ships would take a position west of the town. The *Constitution* would follow the smaller boats toward the harbor and, on Preble's signal, the firing would begin.

By two o'clock, the gunboats were under their own power, advancing on the harbor with sails and oars. At two-thirty, the flagship raised a blue flag, followed by a yellow and blue one, and the third and last, red and blue. This was the signal for the battle to begin, and the *Constitution*, followed by the brigs and schooners, sailed for the harbor.

Fifteen minutes later, the first mortars boomed. Rather than cannonballs, the ships' guns launched hollow projectiles, packed with charges of gunpowder. Flying in a high arc into the city, some exploded in midair, scattering deadly shrapnel in all directions.

The Tripolitans fired back and the American gunboats responded in kind. The *Constitution*, now within a mile of Tripoli's batteries, opened fire with its long guns. The fortress batteries were silenced as the gunners took shelter from the Constitution's broadsides, though, as the big ship sailed past, the Tripolitans resumed firing. "I most sensibly felt the want of another frigate," Preble observed later.[19]

The USS *Constitution* served well, despite taking a cannonball to her mainmast. With Preble standing nearby, another blasted one of the ship's guns; shrapnel shattered a sailor's arm, but Preble escaped with just torn garments.[20] The big frigate and the other larger ships provided covering fire, but the heart of the battle unfolded nearer the waterline. There it was gunboat-to-gunboat and man-to-man.

Within the fortress walls, the American captives could hear little beyond the rumble of guns. On the streets of Tripoli, the townspeople ran for their guns in a scene of excited disorder. At last, the bashaw was getting the full-fledged war he had seemed so keen on provoking for the last three years.

The American gunboats, although outnumbered nineteen to six, bore down on the enemy's boats. Stephen Decatur, captaining one gunboat and accompanied by four other gunboats—the sixth lagged behind—fired at two Tripolitan boats at point-blank range until they retreated behind the line of rocks that protected the inner harbor. Sailing off to find other prey, Decatur's boat, followed by the gunboat commanded by his younger brother James and two other gunboats, headed for a line of five Tripolitan boats moored at the mouth of the harbor's western passage. After a round of American canister shot and musketry, those boats also pulled back into the harbor.

The little American squadron advanced next on a division of nine enemy vessels to the east. None of these fled as Decatur and his men sailed straight at them, looking to get close enough to board. The Americans wished to turn the Tripolitan tactic back upon them, leaping aboard the enemy vessels and fighting hand-to-hand with pistol, saber, pike, and tomahawk. This tactic did not favor the Americans, as a typical two-dozen-man U.S. Navy crew would be met by up to fifty men aboard a Tripolitan ship. But the numbers didn't daunt Decatur: "I always thought we could lick them their own way and give them two to one."[21]

Not long after three o'clock, he had a chance to prove his confidence.

The gunboats closed on the enemy, firing barrage after barrage of round shot. As the Americans neared the westernmost Tripolitan vessel, the enemy fired their pistols but, before they could reload, the Americans clambered from gunwale to gunwale and leapt onto their decks.

Within ten bloody minutes, Decatur's nineteen men had killed sixteen Tripolitans, wounded fifteen others, and taken the remaining five prisoner. Decatur personally lowered the Tripolitan flag.

Meanwhile, Lieutenant James Decatur, Stephen's brother, aimed for the largest of the Tripolitan gunboats and softened up the enemy with intense fire. As his gunboat closed and James Decatur and his men were poised to board, the Tripolitan captain, with a large portion of his crew already dead or wounded by musket and canister fire, ordered his colors struck in surrender.

For a moment, each Decatur brother possessed a prize.

Putting himself at the front of the boarding party, James stepped aboard the captured Tripolitan vessel. As he did so, the treacherous Tripolitan captain shot him at point-blank range.[22] The young lieutenant, struck in the forehead, tumbled into the sea between the two craft. As the American crew pulled their commander from the water, the master of the Tripolitan gunboat ordered his crew to pull for their harbor.

A dishonorable act left a brave officer, his life in the balance, bleeding on the deck.

When Stephen Decatur's boat, towing a captured ship of its own, happened upon James's boat, a short time later, the crew informed Stephen that his younger brother was hovering between life and death.

Suddenly, the thrill of battle was gone from Decatur's eyes, replaced by the cold fury of a man set on revenge. Taking a small crew of eleven men, he set out to chase down the enemy ship that had acted so deceitfully and swore that the murderous captain would find no mercy at his hand. Decatur's crew, some of whom had been part of the *Philadelphia* mission, were determined to follow their leader to hell and back, and proved it in the ensuing fight.

Racing through the water, they managed to spot the very ship they sought and swarmed upon it with a shout.

Decatur went for the captain of the enemy ship, a muscular man of imposing height. The American wielded a pike, a wooden pole with an iron spearhead, long a favorite infantry weapon for close combat. His powerful opponent, avoiding the thrust of Decatur's pike, managed to get one hand, then two, on its wooden shaft. The two men struggled briefly before the stronger Tripolitan wrenched the pike from Decatur's grasp.

As his adversary turned his own weapon against him, Decatur drew his saber to counter the coming blow. Though he deflected the pike, Decatur's blade broke at the hilt.

An instant later, his opponent thrust again, aiming for Decatur's heart. Decatur leapt aside, but the tip of the blade penetrated the flesh of his upper chest. He grappled for the weapon and, as the two men tumbled to the deck, Decatur managed to wrest the weapon from his opponent's grip and pull the blade from his wound.

The pike clattered out of reach.

Their hands now empty of weapons, the two men rolled and wrestled. The Tripolitan reached for a slim dagger that hung at his waist and a Tripolitan sailor, seeing his commander in a life-and-death embrace on the deck, raised his sword to strike Decatur.

The American was as good as dead, but as the Tripolitan's scimitar arced toward Decatur's exposed skull, a sailor named Daniel Frazier, already wounded in the fight, launched himself into the path of the blade, taking the blow for his captain. Frazier sustained a deep head wound, but the captains fought on.

Though weakened by the wound in his bloodied shoulder, Decatur held his opponent's blade away from his throat. With his other hand, he felt for his own pocket—and his pistol. Grasping the gun, he cocked it and, twisting the barrel away from himself, pulled the trigger.

When the ball ripped into his abdomen, the Tripolitan's body went slack.

Decatur had won this contest. But the victory—the Tripolitan gunboat was his—was soon diminished by word of his brother's condition.

By four-thirty Preble, noting a change in the wind, signaled his ships to retire from the action. Within fifteen minutes, all his vessels were out of range of the Tripolitan guns.

As evening fell, the fates of both Daniel Frazier and James Decatur hung in the balance. Despite his own wounds, Stephen Decatur stayed all night at his brother's side. When dawn broke, Frazier was still clinging to life but James's body was committed to the sea. According to his brother's first biographer, Stephen said upon the expiration of his brother, "I would rather see him thus than living with an cloud upon his conduct."[23]

Though another lieutenant suffered severe saber wounds, James Decatur was the only American killed. Just eleven men were wounded, and the man who had sacrificed himself for Decatur, Daniel Frazier, recovered from his wounds. An exact enemy casualty count was unknown, but the dead numbered at least fifty, the wounded perhaps double that.

In two and a half hours of fighting and bombardment, the Tripolitans lost six gunboats. The shore batteries sustained some damage, but the fifty mortar shells thrown into the town had inflicted little damage. Though a good day for Preble, this had been far from an absolute victory. More than exploding mortar shells and a few dead pirates would be required to persuade the bashaw to consider peace.

For weeks, Preble did his considerable best to annoy the Tripolitans from the sea. His fleet bombarded the city from the west on August 7, but the results were disappointing. Most of the bombs landed well away from the bashaw's castle. Preble's forces sustained a painful loss when one of the captured gunboats exploded and killed ten American crewmen.

August 7 was also the day that Preble learned he was being replaced by Commodore Barron. Preble was mortified, though it made sense that the senior officer would take command, and he decided to return to America once the new commodore arrived. But until then he would continue his duty. On the night of August 24, Preble dispatched the gunboats to pound the city. He inflicted little damage on the bashaw's defenses, although, unknown to Preble, a cannonball crashed through one wall of Captain Bainbridge's room. He had been asleep in his bed but the ball ricocheted off another wall before pulling off the prisoner's bedclothes. Cut and bruised by falling masonry, Bainbridge sustained no serious injury, though a deep ankle wound left him limping for some weeks.

Another nighttime bombardment on August 28 sank another gunboat, but with the supply of ammunition running low and Barron expected any day, the fleet needed a new strategy. Preble decided that the USS *Intrepid* would once again take center stage in what was likely his closing scene in the war with Tripoli. If he could not end the war, he might at least shock the bashaw into negotiation.

Since conveying Decatur and his men on their February mission to the captured *Philadelphia*, the *Intrepid* had been a transport, ferrying water and provisions from Syracuse. Now, however, Preble decided to dispatch the former *Mastico* again into the dangers of Tripoli harbor. But this time, the *Intrepid* would not return.

Preble personally supervised the conversion of the little ship into an "infernal machine." Using wooden planks, the squadron's men stowed five tons of powder below her deck. Stacked above on the ship's deck were one hundred thirteen-inch and fifty nine-inch shells, together with iron scraps and pig iron ballast. The ship had become a floating bomb.

The gunners calculated that, after being lit, fuses would give the crew eleven minutes to make their getaway. A small room in the stern of the ship was filled with kindling and other combustibles. It was to be set afire to discourage Tripolitan boarders as the Americans made their escape in the two fastest rowing boats in the squadron, pulling for the harbor entrance and the *Nautilus* just beyond.

The fleet continued an on-again, off-again bombardment of Tripoli into early September, waiting for perfect conditions. Then, on September 3, at eight o'clock in the evening, the *Intrepid* slipped her cable and sailed for Tripoli.

No moon lit her way and, powered by a moderate breeze, she glided swiftly toward the harbor. The *Nautilus* accompanied her to a distance of some seven hundred yards from the western mouth of the harbor, then stopped to wait at a distance.

The *Intrepid*'s Captain Richard Somers and his crew were on their own in the starry night. Their mission was dangerous—their ship was a tinderbox, after all—but they carried another burden. The blockaded Tripolitans were probably running low on gunpowder. If, by some misfortune, the *Intrepid* were to fall into their hands, its large stores of ammunition could prolong the war. Knowing this must not happen, Somers had asked that no volunteer accompany him who would not be willing, in the event the enemy should board the *Intrepid*, to "put a match to the magazine, and blow themselves and their enemies up together."[24]

The men aboard the *Nautilus* watched as the *Intrepid* made way toward Tripoli. As the minutes passed, the smaller ship, barely discernible in the dim light, seemed to be entering the harbor passage. Then two gunshots were heard. Were they alarm guns fired from the Tripolitan batteries? Silence followed, and the crew of the *Nautilus* waited anxiously.

For ten minutes, the only sound to be heard was the lapping of the waves.

Then, at 9:47 p.m. according to the *Constitution*'s log, a blaze of light suddenly illuminated the sky and the towers, minarets, and castellated walls of Tripoli. An instant later, a deafening explosion of sound struck the American ships, its concussion shaking even the *Constitution* six miles out to sea.

A different, more profound silence fell.

The lookouts on the *Nautilus* strained their eyes, hoping to see Somers and his men stroking for safety in their two boats. From his more distant anchorage, Preble studied the sky anxiously, praying to spot a rocket, the agreed-upon signal that Somers and his men had escaped the harbor. The sky remained an unbroken black.

With the sunrise, the three ships Preble sent to stand offshore reported that the fort appeared undamaged, the Tripolitan navy intact.

Finally the remains of her hull were spotted, the keel and ribs of the *Intrepid* grounded just outside the rocky barrier. The ship had exploded well short of the bashaw's castle, for reasons that could not be known (a sniper's bullet? an accidental spark? the powder touched off by Somers when a Tripolitan boarding party neared?). Even before the bashaw permitted Captain Bainbridge to view the remains of "six persons in a most mangled and burnt condition lying on the shore,"[25] it became clear there could be no survivors.

Preble's final attempt to persuade the bashaw to surrender had failed.

THE NEW COMMODORE

On September 9, the USS *President* and USS *Constellation* were sighted as Preble's flagship cruised off the Tripoli coast. Preble ordered his pennant struck. With the arrival of Commodore Samuel Barron, Preble officially ceased being squadron commander, and his thoughts turned to home.

"Commodore Barron's arrival to supersede me in the command of the fleet has determined me to return," a dispirited Preble wrote to Mary.[26] Yet before departing, he would spend many hours in conference with Barron. And in attendance at some of those briefings would be William Eaton, who had sailed with Barron. A favored topic of conversation between the three men was Eaton's proposal to aid Hamet Qaramanli.

Eaton helped assure Preble that, although he was being displaced by Barron, he could go home with his head held high. Although Edward Preble would not remain in the Mediterranean to see the war through to its close, in his time of service in the Maghreb he had established a negotiated peace with Morocco. During his service as commodore, his men had demonstrated a new and remarkable fighting prowess. Even if he had not achieved the larger victory he hoped for, Preble's service in the region was another honorable chapter in his distinguished career.

When Preble did finally arrive in Washington on March 4, 1805, he received a well-deserved hero's welcome. Despite his disappointment with his own performance, there was no way to term his Barbary tour anything but a success. He'd taken the fight to Tripoli, destroyed pirate vessels, and made sure the *Philadelphia* wasn't used against the United States. Recognizing his achievements, the president welcomed him as an honored guest, and he was celebrated at the home of the secretary of state, as well as at dinners in Philadelphia, Trenton, and Boston. Congress ordered a medal struck with his likeness. For his valiant efforts and sound strategies off the Barbary Coast, he had become an American legend.

The Americans were still riding high on Preble's and Decatur's successes, but there was one fact they couldn't ignore: though America's sea victories had won respect and concessions from some of the Barbary states, Tripoli was still unrepentantly hostile. In the months that followed Preble's return, the president and his advisers began to turn their hopes toward Eaton's plan. Perhaps a land war and accompanying coup could finally solve the Tripoli problem.

CHAPTER 14

Opening a New Front

It grates me mortally when I see a lazy Turk reclining at his
ease upon an embroidered sofa, with one Christian slave to
hold his pipe, another to hold his coffee, and a third to fan
away the flies.

—**William Eaton**[1]

Jefferson's government left the decision of whether to help Hamet
in the hands of their men in the Mediterranean. The chief diplomat and the commodore, Lear and Barron, would have to approve Eaton's efforts if he was to move forward. Accordingly, on their
transatlantic crossing, William Eaton had presented Commodore
Samuel Barron with impassioned arguments for his scheme.

Eaton's lawyerly arguments were strong. He maintained that
only a ground campaign would force Yusuf into accepting a peace on
American terms. He pointed out that the Americans most familiar
with the politics of the region, Richard O'Brien and James Leander
Cathcart, had endorsed the idea of restoring Hamet as bashaw. On
arrival in the Mediterranean, they found that Captain Preble had, too.

Even if Barron remained vague about how it was to be done, he could hardly reject the collective advice of these experienced Barbary men. With some reluctance, he agreed to provide Eaton transport to go in search of the deposed bashaw.

But not all the American officials stationed in the Mediterranean and involved in Barbary affairs thought the mission a good one. Chief Consul Tobias Lear, the region's most important representative of the Department of State, complained that Hamet lacked the force or influence needed to make him helpful to the Americans. But it is difficult to know whether Lear's objections were based more on his doubts about Hamet's strength or on fears that the plan would diminish his own power. During Commodore Preble's time, Lear's role in America's foreign relations had been minor. Preble thought military strength, not negotiations, were the means to peace, relegating Lear's work to the background. With the arrival of Barron, especially now that the commodore had suddenly been confined to his cabin, sick with liver disease, Lear saw the door might be open for him to wield more influence. Eaton's plan, also based on military strength instead of negotiations, might close that door again.

MARINES

Despite Colonel Lear's doubts, Eaton's plan received approval. He was authorized to find Hamet, negotiate with him, and raise an Arab army to help restore the rightful bashaw to power. These orders in hand, in November 1804, Eaton sailed for Egypt aboard the USS *Argus*. Built to hold 142 men, the snug ship easily took aboard

Eaton's tiny army, which, at that moment, consisted solely of Eaton, 2 U.S. Navy midshipmen, and 8 U.S. Marines.

If Eaton's band fell far short of the army he hoped to build, he still maintained high hopes—and one reason was the presence of the Marines and their leader, Lieutenant Presley O'Bannon. Eaton needed such men, skilled fighters on land and sea.

Lithe and lean with red hair, O'Bannon was popular as a lively violin player who could dance as well as he could fiddle a tune. He was also a born fighter. A young man from the heart of Virginia's Piedmont region, he was eager to defend American interests in an exotic climate. The Marines' reputation for toughness and tenacity, along with the promise of adventure coupled with patriotic duty, had attracted the naturally spirited young man, and he had enthusiastically embraced Eaton's plan.

Eaton's ten men amounted to a small start, of course, but these committed young fighters, Eaton believed, would soon be supplemented by Hamet's larger army in Egypt. Hamet's loyal followers could also be reinforced by hiring mercenaries and, thanks to his years in North Africa, Eaton understood the value of local soldiers, men acclimated to the unique demands of desert living. He also felt confident that disaffected Tripolitans would flock to Hamet's side once he marched back into his country. A fine team was in the making.

FINDING THE TRAIL

Before Eaton and his Marines could help Hamet, though, they had to find him—and in 1804 no one seemed to know where Sidi Hamet

Qaramanli was hiding. When the rumor had circulated, in July 1803, that Bashaw Yusuf had dispatched assassins to kill him in the eastern Tripolitan city of Derne, Hamet had run for his life, fleeing to Egypt. Reports indicated that the thin, soft-spoken former bashaw remained there. But where, exactly? Forced to be on the move out of fear of his brother's agents, he seemed to have disappeared into the sands of the Sahara.

Eaton's first port of call in November 1804 was the ancient city of Alexandria, Egypt. On arrival, the Americans found a country divided. Albanian Turks held power on behalf of the Ottoman Empire, but their rule extended only to Cairo. Farther upriver were the rebellious Mamelukes, heirs to an Egyptian dynasty that dated to medieval times. Meanwhile both French and British colonial forces had, in recent years, been stationed in the country. As if the competing political interests were not enough, Egypt was in the midst of a famine, a result of a scant harvest. "Egypt has no master," Eaton noted a few days into his visit. "Pale Wretchedness and dumb melancholy stalk here!"[2]

Eaton recognized that he needed Egyptian help if he was to find Hamet. Accordingly, he befriended the natives and, over candies and coffee, he learned that the man he sought was upriver. However, Eaton's blood ran cold on being told that Hamet had joined forces with the Mamelukes, the sworn enemies of the Ottoman Empire and, more immediately, the powers that controlled the mouth of the river. Supposing he found Hamet, how was Eaton to extract him and his supporters, as they would have to travel through Ottoman territory? That would require a miraculous act of diplomacy, but even so, the intrepid William Eaton, having persuaded a president, a government, and the U.S. Navy to support his scheme, gamely headed up the Nile to Cairo. There he would next make his case to the viceroy of Egypt.

MAKING FRIENDS WITH EGYPT

Eaton's expedition sailed south, the waters of the Nile guiding them farther into Egypt. Evidence of political instability was everywhere. One village had been raided by a roving band of deserters from the Turkish army just days before who had destroyed anything valuable or growing. At one town, the Americans were mistaken for British soldiers, and the locals "flocked around with demonstrations of joy," offering to help any army that would protect them from the marauding forces.[3]

Letters from the British consul gained Eaton an audience with the Egyptian viceroy in Cairo. Because it was Ramadan, the holy month of fasting when no refreshments could be served during the day, Viceroy Ahmed Khorshid invited Eaton to call upon him at nine o'clock in the evening. Eaton was conducted from the British consulate to the viceroy's citadel in a torch-lit procession, escorted by servants and dignitaries and six lavishly decorated Arabian horses. He looked upon the spectators lining the streets of the mile-and-a-half route, an enormous crowd "curious to see *the men who had come from the new world*."[4] His welcome was worthy of a great visitor.

The viceroy himself seemed most interested to learn about the United States, and asked Eaton many question about America, the "situation and extent of our territory; date of our independence; nations with whom we were at peace or war; productions and commerce of the country? &c &c." The two men sat in a large hall, Eaton reported, which "surpassed in magnificence everything I have ever seen of its kind." Seated side by side, they shared an embroidered purple couch with damask cushions and sat drinking coffee, smoking pipes, and eating sherbet.

Then the viceroy dismissed everyone from his presence except Eaton and an interpreter. The pleasantries ended as the ruler observed, "[Y]our visit to this country at so critical a moment must have something more for its object than mere gratification of curiosity."

Eaton went straight to the heart of the matter. Replying in French, which the Turkish interpreter understood better than English, Eaton described "our intercourse and relation with Tripoli." He explained that the current bashaw of Tripoli had declared the war, which the Americans wanted to end. Although often criticized for being blunt, Eaton demonstrated great subtlety in winning the viceroy over to his plan. He flattered the Egyptian, contrasting his magnanimity with the tyranny of the Barbary princes.

He argued that Islam and Christianity had many commonalities, hinting that the Egyptian could ally with him as a matter of faith. "I touched upon the affinity of principle between the Islam and Americans religion. Both taught the existence and supremacy of *one* God . . . both enjoyed the universal exercise of humanity, and both forbade unnecessary bloodshed."

The viceroy had to agree: indeed, these were maxims of his faith. Eaton pressed on.

He told the viceroy that he was seeking Hamet: "I declared that we sought in his province a legitimate sovereign of Tripoli: who had been treacherously driven from his government and country; in whose good faith we could place reliance, and whom we intended to restore to his throne." And he explained that America had no interest in occupying Tripoli: "we do not unsheathe the sword for conquest nor for spoil, but to vindicate our rights." The United States sought only to defend its own citizens and interests from unwarranted attack.

The viceroy recognized the American as a worthy brother and, "by an inclination of his head, [the viceroy] signified assent and promised to send couriers in search of Hamet Bashaw."

Eaton's persuasive words had won him an ally in the search for Hamet. Now, however, he must wait for the man to be found.

The viceroy was true to his word, and he dispatched messengers upriver to find Hamet. Eaton, too, sent a mercenary to discover the whereabouts of the missing man. Several nervous weeks passed before the messengers located the former bashaw, but they delivered Eaton's message to him on January 3. Five days later, Eaton received Hamet's eager reply.

The former bashaw was ready for the expedition, confident "that God will aid us in establishing peace and tranquility."[5] On February 5, 1805, Eaton and Hamet, who had met years earlier in Tunis, were reunited outside Cairo.

On first sight, Hamet struck no one as a powerful prince. His cheeks were pockmarked, his chin and lips obscured by a long beard. On meeting him, one American captain had pronounced Hamet a "mild, amiable man [who] would be perfectly friendly and Peaceable toward us."[6] Though a sympathetic figure, he possessed no great personal magnetism, and no one described him as a warrior. When his brother had taken the throne in 1795, Hamet had seemed incapable of fighting back, and almost a decade later he still lived in exile, separated from his wife and four children, who remained under house arrest in Tripoli.

If Hamet was indecisive and uninspiring, Eaton also recognized him as someone he could mold, someone he could persuade. But before they could embark on the great mission Eaton envisioned, one more delicate negotiation needed to be completed.

Taking it upon himself to represent the United States of America, Eaton negotiated with the former bashaw concerning their respective promises. Hamet needed to be sure the Americans would support him. Eaton needed assurances that Hamet would treat Americans well once he was in power. Their conversations yielded a formal agreement.

The treaty opened with one line—"GOD IS INFINITE"—followed by an oath of friendship between the government of the United States and the one to be reestablished by Hamet. Per the contract, the United States would provide the force, funds, and supplies to restore the throne to Hamet. In return, the once and future bashaw would ask no ransom for the release of the men of the *Philadelphia*. Hamet also promised to deliver Yusuf and Admiral Murat Rais to the Americans. Signed by Eaton and Hamet, the document was witnessed by Presley O'Bannon and the British consul.

With the treaty in place, the plan that William Eaton had been shaping for more than three years was about to unfold. America, pounding Tripoli from the sea, would soon be continuing the attack on land. Together, Eaton and Hamet would raise a mercenary army that would join the Marines for a historic land march across more than five hundred miles of rocky desert to Derne, Tripoli's second-largest city. Once Derne had fallen, they would march west to Benghazi. They would capture that city, and then U.S. warships would carry them the last four hundred miles to take Tripoli. It was a bold plan—but despite the doubts of Lear and others, Eaton felt confident that it could work.

CHAPTER 15

Win in the Desert or Die in the Desert

'Tis done, the hornéd crescent falls!
The Star-flag flouts the broken walls!

—John Greenleaf Whittier, "Derne," 1850

On March 6, 1805, the trek began. Four hundred men set out from Alexandria, their goal—to change the history of the Barbary Coast. Among their number were just ten Americans, including Lieutenant O'Bannon, a midshipman, a Marine sergeant, and six Marine privates. Hamet brought along ninety Tripolitans. The rest were hired mercenaries, mostly Greek and Arab cavalrymen and foot soldiers. It was a long caravan, led from the front with martial efficiency but diminishing to pack animals with supplies well to the rear.

Newly self-declared "General, and Commander in Chief of the land forces," William Eaton marched proudly in uniform, epaulets on his shoulders, his hat decorated with lace, his buttons and spurs polished brass. One of the oddest—and yet most effective—military campaigns in American history had begun, with General Eaton leading the charge.

UPS AND DOWNS

The march to Derne had barely started before a mutiny jeopardized the whole trip. After just three days of marching along the coast, the camel wranglers hired to guide the pack animals demanded to be paid in advance. When an irresolute Hamet did nothing, Eaton threatened to abandon the expedition. The mutineers quieted, and the little revolutionary army marched on, averaging roughly twenty miles a day.

As they marched, Eaton marveled over the beautiful but hostile desert. The men passed incredible scenes, both man-made and natural. "Passed some vestiges of ancient fortifications," Eaton noted on March 14 as they camped on the high ridge that marked the boundary between Egypt and Tripoli. The sights were inspiring, but the weather was less so. The long column soon encountered incessant rain blowing in from the coast that soaked the men and their supplies. Temperatures rose to almost 100 degrees Fahrenheit by day and plunged to near freezing at night. The Sahara was not making Eaton's task easy.

At intervals, the Arabs who owned the camels made new demands. They looted the food supplies, and the caravan grew shorter as some of the Arabs deserted. During the day, O'Bannon and his Marines, imposing in their blue uniforms with scarlet collars and trimmings, and distinguished by their firm and decided conduct, helped prevent further mutinies. After sundown, O'Bannon gained popularity among the Americans, Turks, Arabs, and Greeks alike. He had brought his violin along, and he would play for the camp—for perhaps the first time, the strains of Irish and Appalachian fiddle tunes echoed across the North African desert's rocky terrain.

After almost a month of marching, Eaton's army encountered a large camp of several thousand Bedouins. "We were the first Christians ever seen by these wild people," Eaton observed. Just as he had hoped, the ranks of his little army began to swell. Eighty mounted warriors joined from the Bedouins and, by early April, Eaton counted "between six and seven hundred fighting men on the ground, exclusive of followers of the camp and Bedouin families, who inclusively make a body of about twelve hundred people."[1] As it marched across the plateau that overlooked the seas, Eaton's army was becoming more formidable, ready to take on the official Tripolitan forces.

REBELLION

Good fortune was not to last. By mid-April, the company's food supply had dwindled to just six days' rations of rice, the bread and meat exhausted. The marchers had already slaughtered a camel for meat, and the Marines sold their brass buttons to local Bedouins for a few dates. Wild fennel and sorrel were harvested when they could be found, but everyone remained hungry. The procession came to a standstill when the sheiks commanding the Arabs in the force refused to march until a messenger sent to Bomba returned with assurances that Isaac Hull, in command of the USS *Argus*, awaited them with fresh supplies.

Eaton refused to halt. He saw the choice as between famine and fatigue. Bomba was ninety miles away and, he believed, to remain in place in the heat of the desert would amount to suicide. They needed to push on—and he ordered all rations stopped until they did.

The bashaw walked out of camp, refusing to take sides in the dispute, but the Arab mercenaries prepared to raid the provisions tent. Reading their intentions, Eaton ordered O'Bannon and the Marines to form a line. The armed, uniformed men stood their ground, immobile as a "body of about two hundred advanced in full charge"[2] in a frenzied panic driven by hunger, desperation, and distrust. Amazed by O'Bannon's men's resolute refusal to so much as blink in light of the approaching mob, the Arabs stopped, then withdrew. The sheiks were about to order their men to shoot the American officers, but just as the cry went up to draw their weapons, a few of Hamet's officers called out in Arabic, "For God's sake, do not fire! The Christians are our friends!" O'Bannon and company again stood firm, unmoving.

Hamet's officers then rushed forward, their sabers drawn, and drove the mutineers back. A crisis averted, at least for the night, Eaton vented his frustrations in his journal. Despite apparent gains in mutual understanding with their Arab comrades, Eaton noted, "We find it almost impossible to inspire these wild bigots with confidence in us, or to persuade them that, being Christians, we can be otherwise than enemies to Mussulmen. We have a difficult undertaking!"[3]

Things got no easier when, a week later, the caravan stumbled

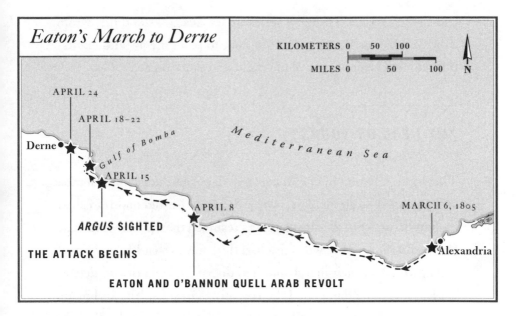

into Bomba, wild with hunger and thirst, and eager to rest with full bellies and no fear of starvation. They found Eaton's often-repeated promise—that American ships awaited the army at Bomba—proved untrue: there were no American ships in the harbor. The Arabs and Bedouins alike immediately declared their intentions to leave in the morning, to countermarch home. The Americans could go forth toward whatever folly they desired, but they would do so alone.

"All began now to think of the means of individual safety," Eaton wrote. "I went off with my Christians, and kept up fires upon a high mountain in our rear all night." He desperately hoped that huge hill-top fire would not only provide security for their camp but also signal any American ships in the area, because native scouts had sworn to their presence just a few days earlier.

The plan worked. At eight o'clock the following morning a sail was sighted. "Capt. Hull had seen our smokes and stood in," wrote a relieved Eaton. "Language is too poor to paint the joy and exultation which this messenger of life excited in every breast."[4]

"MY HEAD OR YOURS"

The *Argus*, followed by the *Hornet* two days later, sailed into Bomba and unloaded its goods. For a week the army feasted and refreshed itself until, on April 23, the marchers resumed their progress toward Derne. En route again, word reached the caravan that Bashaw Yusuf had heard about their march and had dispatched an army to defend Derne. The news dampened the recently buoyant spirits and made poor Hamet fear for himself and his family. "I thought the Bashaw [Hamet] wished himself back in Egypt,"[5] Eaton observed. Still, Hamet rallied. The little army pressed on and, on April 25, made camp on a ridge overlooking its destination.

The next morning, Eaton sent a letter to the governor of Derne. "I want no territory," his message read. "With me is advancing the legitimate Sovereign of your country—give us a passage through your city, and for the supplies of which we shall have need, you will receive fair compensation. . . . I shall see you tomorrow in a way of your choice."[6]

By early afternoon, Eaton had his reply. "The flag of truce was sent back to me with this laconic answer, 'My head or yours!'"[7]

As the sun rose over the Sahara on April 27, Bashaw Hamet, William Eaton, Presley O'Bannon, and their unlikely army of mercenaries, midshipmen, Marines, Greeks, Arabs, and Bedouins—a brave band of misfits—prepared to storm the city gates.

CAPTURING THE CASTLE

Looking down upon the town of Derne on April 27, 1805, General William Eaton concocted the plan of attack.

Derne was nestled into a crook of the Mediterranean coast. The governor's palace sat upon an easterly spit of land that jutted into the blue waters of the bay. A ten-inch howitzer had been mounted on its terrace. Word having reached the provincial capital that an invading force approached, the town had been armed with a battery of eight guns aimed out to sea. To the landward, loopholes had been opened in houses along the city walls to form a line of defense.

Eaton's plan called for an attack on Derne on three fronts. First, from the sea, the guns aboard the three American ships would bombard the city. Second, using field guns sent by Barron, Eaton and his men would fire upon the walls of the city from the southeast. Finally, a wave of men led by Hamet Qaramanli would descend on the rear of the town from the west.

On the morning of April 27, the *Nautilus* brought Eaton's guns to shore. There a narrow beach immediately gave way to a steep climb, but the task of hauling a heavy carronade up the slope with block and tackle proved time-consuming. Eager to get to the coming fight, Eaton decided to settle for just one artillery piece.

Finally, at one-thirty on the afternoon of April 27, the assault began. From a distance of half a mile out to sea, the *Argus* and the *Nautilus* began firing into the town. From their vantage on the hillside, O'Bannon and his men maintained a steady musket fire, accompanied by round shot from the carronade. With the *Hornet* positioned

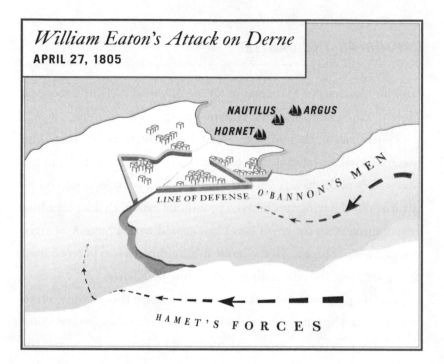

in the bay to fire on the city from a distance of just one hundred yards,
Derne was taking heavy bombardment.

At first, the attack seemed to go well. Within forty-five minutes,
Derne's harbor guns fell silent. Under heavy fire from the U.S. Navy
ships, the Tripolitans operating the harbor guns had withdrawn and
moved to reinforce the defenders of the more vulnerable south wall.

Eaton's cannoneers kept up their fire until a cannonball shattered
their rammer, the long wooden tool used to drive the shot and powder wad down the bore of the large gun. No longer able to load and
fire the gun, the men around O'Bannon and Eaton were thrown into
confusion.

Thinking fast, Eaton saw but one alternative: he ordered a charge down the hill, directly into the teeth of the enemy's defense. The odds were not in his favor but he remained undaunted.

"We rushed forward against a host of savages more than ten to our one."[8] On horseback, Eaton led the charge at a gallop, an intimidating sight as he swung his custom-made scimitar over his head. By some miracle, he was not injured by the enemy's gunfire, though he would find five bullet holes in his robes.[9]

On the other side of town, Hamet and his troops occupied an old castle and awaited their signal. Eaton had instructed the Tripolitan to lead his force of more than seven hundred men, some on foot, others on horseback, and attack the city via a deep ravine southwest of Derne. Sheiks sympathetic to the former bashaw had advised that he could expect support from most of the population in that part of the city. Other horsemen in Hamet's force were to take positions in the surrounding hills to the rear, ready to cut off any Tripolitan forces attempting to retreat from the city.

As a dense cloud of blue smoke rose from the harbor, a delighted Eaton had seen Hamet's horsemen swooping down to the city. Knowing that Hamet's army was fighting fiercely on the other side of the city emboldened him for the daring charge of the city walls. Cannon fire from the ships offered cover as Eaton, O'Bannon, and their men crossed the beach, but the men still faced volleys of musket balls from the ramparts.

One of O'Bannon's seven Marines fell, seriously wounded. Another took a bullet to the chest, dying immediately. Then Eaton himself took a musket ball to the left wrist. Yet the wave of men and their flashing bayonets continued their charge.

To the surprise of the small brigade of invaders, the city's defenders began to retreat into the city as the Americans approached. The frontal assault produced a growing panic. The ragged fire from behind the walls ceased, and the Tripolitan defenders melted into the dizzying maze of the city's twisting streets and stacked houses. The retreating army managed only sporadic fire as they retreated.

With Eaton wounded, O'Bannon took full command. Breaching the city's walls, he led the charge directly to the oceanfront guns. There, after lowering the bashaw's ensign, O'Bannon planted the American flag on the ramparts. He then turned the enemy's own guns on them—abandoned in a rush during the naval bombardment, many were still loaded, powdered, and ready to fire. In a matter of minutes, the Americans held the high ground and the artillery.

Meanwhile, at the other end of town, Hamet's flag could now be seen flying from the governor's palace. After years of planning, months of preparations, and a fifty-two-day march that covered more than five hundred miles, the city had fallen in the short span of two and a half hours.

All told, there were fourteen dead and wounded among the contingent of Americans and Greeks led by Eaton and O'Bannon. Two of the dead were O'Bannon's Marines. The number of casualties among Hamet's party and the Tripolitan forces was not recorded but totaled in the hundreds.

Eaton was elated. His plan had worked thus far, and an army of fewer than a thousand men had overrun a fighting force of four thousand. The governor of Derne was still at large—he found refuge in a mosque—but Eaton felt certain the victory would win many Tripolitans to Hamet's side—and it would demonstrate to the world that the Americans were not to be trifled with. Eaton had proved that distance was no barrier to the Americans and put the world on notice that Hamet, the rightful ruler of their country, had his sights set on regaining his throne and his family. Rejoicing at the prospect of victory, Hamet is said to have offered his sword to O'Bannon as a token of his thanks.

Word of the fall of Derne was bound to anger and panic the bashaw. Hamet and the Americans were coming for him, and Bashaw Yusuf knew it. But Eaton's victory would be stymied by a surprising source.

CHAPTER 16

Endgame

Our captive countrymen have been restored to the bosom of
their country, peace has been made on honorable terms. . . .
We have got all we wanted.

—*National Intelligencer,* October 25, 1805

With Eaton's resounding victory in Derne, a military victory in Tripoli seemed within reach. But Tobias Lear had other plans. He wanted a diplomatic deal, and a deal is what he made.

Lear had opposed launching the assault on Derne from the first, and he fully expected the mission to fail. In his mind, Eaton was a failed consul, a man playing at being soldier, even a "madman."[1] His presence in the region undercut Lear's diplomatic authority, and Lear feared that a military victory would ruin his chances for brokering a diplomatic peace.

Now Lear received news of Eaton's success. Lear's prediction had been wrong, but he was determined not to let the news go to waste. With a little quick thinking, Eaton's victory could be leveraged, not for an absolute victory, but for a brokered peace.

A few weeks before the attack on Derne, Bashaw Yusuf had showed signs of wanting to make peace—but only on his terms. In return for $200,000, he promised to release Captain Bainbridge and the men of the USS *Philadelphia*. Though desperate for a deal, Lear recognized the offer for the extortion it was and rejected it.

Then the news of the capture of Derne arrived—and Lear saw his great chance. He felt certain that the news of Hamet's victory would strike fear into Bashaw Yusuf—and he was right.

Although Lear did not know it, when the Tripolitan leader heard of the fall of Derne on May 21, he was terrified. "The Bashaw was so much agitated at the news of the approach of his brother, that he . . . declared, that if it was in his power now to make peace and give up the American prisoners, he would gladly do it, without the consideration of money. . . ," one Philadelphia captive reported. "He heartily repented for not accepting the terms of peace last offered."[2] Had Lear acted with strength, he might have been granted all of his demands without having to pay.

Instead, Lear underestimated the effect of Eaton's victory on the Barbary powers. Aboard the USS *Constitution*, Lear took what he thought was a hard position: he offered $60,000 in payment for the freedom of the *Philadelphia*'s captives and refused to go ashore until the bashaw agreed to his terms.

The relieved bashaw saw a chance to save his throne. He accepted the deal, and by June 3, the terms were agreed upon. Two days later, Colonel Lear went into the city and was welcomed into the palace. Peace was declared and the prisoners freed—but the achievement was tainted. Lear had paid for the release of American prisoners, and even worse, he had betrayed Eaton and Hamet. As part of the deal, Lear had promised that all American forces would evacuate Derne.

THE END OF THE ROAD

Unaware of Lear's negotiation, General Eaton, Hamet, and their men stood firm as their enemies counterattacked. The governor of Derne had fled, taking with him intelligence about the invading forces, and he was using the information as he struck back at the Americans. As the attacks continued, Eaton feared that either his supplies or the nerves of his men would give out. He noted in his journal that the apprehensive Hamet tended to become "deeply agitated."[3] The brave liberators of Derne held the city securely, but they could not hold out indefinitely without supplies and reinforcements.

Yet Eaton could do little but wait for the American response to his call for support. When the response came, it was not the men, munitions, and other aid he had requested. Instead, he got a letter advising him that the peace process had begun and no further advancement of his army would be necessary or supported.

Eaton was stunned.

Even more stunning was the accompanying order for him to abandon Derne and come home. The flabbergasted Eaton, who had fully expected to carry his fight to Benghazi and even Tripoli, was told to give up the ground purchased with his men's blood and to renege on his promises to Hamet.

Outraged, Eaton immediately wrote a long letter to Commodore Barron. He argued that a withdrawal would be a dangerous sign of weakness in a region that respected only strength. "Certainly they, and perhaps the world, will place an unjust construction on this retreat: at any rate it is a retreat—and a retreat of Americans!"[4]

Rather than withdraw from Derne as he waited for a reply to his letter to Barron, Eaton remained in place. He refused to accept that he would be forced to return hard-won ground to the pirates. Then, on June 11, another ship sailed into Derne harbor bringing a new message.

This time, it was the USS *Constellation*, and the dispatches that came ashore included one from Tobias Lear, dated five days earlier. Lear credited "the heroic bravery of our few countrymen at Derne . . . [that] made a deep impression on the Bashaw." The result had been a formal end to the war, but word of Lear's treaty was a blow to Eaton from which he would never recover. He was again told to abandon his prize and even his hopes of helping Hamet. This time Eaton saw that with the treaty in place, there was no getting around orders.

Even as the victor at Derne accepted that he had little choice but to leave, Eaton realized that withdrawal would be a delicate matter. If word leaked that the American forces were preparing to depart, enemy forces might be emboldened to attack. That meant the Americans must leave in secrecy.

Behaving as if nothing had changed, Eaton spent the next day inspecting the garrison and issuing orders as usual. Then, at eight o'clock in the evening, he posted the Marines in a conspicuous place, hoping they would serve as a decoy. Over the next several hours, the rest of the small American force was ferried to the *Constellation* as unobtrusively as possible. Eaton then summoned the outraged and brokenhearted Hamet, who reluctantly joined the retreat because he had no choice but to accept that pursuing the battle without

American help was impossible. The Marines, the officers, and Eaton went last. There could be no farewells, no ceremony. Just a quiet exit, a retreat that felt shameful.

When Hamet's Arab allies discovered that the Americans had left, they panicked. Once the bashaw's men learned the news, they would visit their fury on those left behind. Humiliated and betrayed, the sympathetic Arabs ran for the mountains, abandoning the town. In Tripoli there might be peace, but the citizens of Derne who had embraced Hamet would pay a heavy price for their support.

The resourceful William Eaton had won—against all odds—a stunning victory in Derne. And yet as Eaton sailed away, he saw his chance for greater glory—and for an even greater victory for his country—wash away with the tides that brought word of the treaty. Now he simply wished to go home. Listless and defeated, he wrote to Commodore John Rodgers, "I have no reasons for remaining any longer in this sea."[5]

A Senate committee would later investigate what had unfolded in Tripoli that June. Eaton's old friend Senator Timothy Pickering would offer a blistering condemnation of Lear, describing his conduct as "nothing but the basest treachery on the basest principles."[6] The committee strongly criticized the treaty as an "inglorious deed."[7] Yet the Senate still mustered the required two-thirds majority to ratify the Treaty of Peace and Amity between the United States and Tripoli. Whatever the disagreements about the way in which it had come to pass, the peace, at that moment, became an established fact.

CHAPTER 17

Fair Winds and Following Seas

Peace has been made on honorable terms.

—*National Intelligencer,* November 6, 1805

The new Barbary peace truly was a victory, though an incomplete one. For President Jefferson, who got wind of Lear's treaty on September 6, 1805, the end of the conflict with Tripoli was a great relief. The war that had dogged his administration for more than four years was finally at an end—and it had ended Jefferson's way.

The *National Intelligencer* proclaimed victory. "Our captive countrymen have been restored to the bosom of their country. . . . We have got what we wanted."[1] Indeed, the terms of the treaty stipulated that in the future, captives would not be made slaves but would, in effect, be given the status of prisoners of war. American shipping could flow freely again. The two most essential goals in declaring war had been accomplished.

The country cheered the heroes as they returned to the United

States. In mid-September William Bainbridge arrived, already cleared of blame for the loss of the USS *Philadelphia*. He stepped off the ship along with 117 of his officers and crewmen and they were feted with awards, honors, and a warm welcome. Other returning captains and captives were paraded down main streets and toasted as heroes, too. The Virginia General Assembly honored U.S. Marine Lieutenant Presley O'Bannon, presenting him with a curved sword modeled after the Mameluke scimitar.

A complete victory over the Barbary pirates would come under another president, but for now America had much to be grateful for. The murky ending of the Barbary War didn't take away from the fact that America had stood up to the pirates, something that most of the more established European nations hadn't been willing to do. America had held firm and fought, and now the young nation's navy had the experience it would need to take on Britain in the War of 1812. Like the Barbary War, that war would begin with devastating losses but end with a huge leap in respect from the world.

In prevailing off the Barbary Coast, the United States proved that it would not only go to war for its own interests but would do what it could for oppressed citizens of other nations. Despite Lear's betrayal of Hamet, the American government did not let him down completely. Bringing a little pressure to bear, the Americans were able to free his wife and four children and reunite the family. Granted a $200-a-month payment by Congress, Hamet would end his life in exile in Egypt, dying in 1811. His brother, Yusuf Qaramanli, ruled as bashaw until 1832, when he stepped down to make way for his son Ali II; Yusuf died in 1838.

Tobias Lear kept his job. He would remain consul general to the Barbary states despite the disapproval of his treaty by many back in

Washington. Yet he was not a happy man. He left no note when he took his own life with a pistol shot in 1816.

Richard O'Brien and his wife Elizabeth lived a quiet life after returning to the United States. The O'Briens had five children, including a son named George Africanus, in honor of the continent where Richard had spent ten years in captivity and almost as many again in service to his country. O'Brien died in Washington, D.C., in 1824.

James Leander Cathcart would be appointed to diplomatic posts in Madeira, an island chain off the western coast of Portugal, and in Cádiz, Spain, before returning to the United States. He died in Washington, D.C., in 1843, but his journals and other writings were later collected in *The Captives: Eleven Years a Prisoner in Algiers* (1899).

William Eaton returned to America a national war hero for his role in winning America's first battle on foreign soil. In recognition of his service, the Commonwealth of Massachusetts awarded him ten thousand acres of land in the Maine Territory. In 1807, claims he put before Congress for expenses incurred in the Barbary campaign eventually brought him a windfall of $12,636, but by then his body had begun to betray him. He suffered from gout, and too many tankards bought by admirers took a toll. As his health declined, he penned his life story and collected his journals, knowing they would be published posthumously. By the time the volume appeared as *The Life of the Late Gen. William Eaton,* in 1813, the forty-seven-year-old Eaton had been dead two years.

The names *Philadelphia*, *Intrepid*, and *Constitution* had become well known to readers of American newspapers during the Barbary War. The commodore most closely associated with their

Barbary exploits, Edward Preble, lived until just 1807, succumbing, at age forty-six, to consumption. But his reputation would survive him. Pope Pius VII reportedly said Decatur had done more for the cause of Christianity in an hour than the nations of Christendom ever had. And his name gained further luster in the next decade when several of the officers who fought for him—"Preble's Boys," as they would later come to be known—served with distinction in the War of 1812.

William Bainbridge won a measure of redemption for his twin failures with the *George Washington* and the *Philadelphia* off the Barbary Coast. Though later wounded in both legs in a battle with a British ship, Bainbridge managed to remain upright, commanding the USS *Constitution* to victory in a memorable sea battle with the HMS *Java*. Surviving his injuries, he would live to age fifty-nine, dying peacefully in his bed in 1833.

President Thomas Jefferson spent his retirement at his beloved home in Monticello, where both his wife and daughter Polly were buried. With his health declining, he was bedridden in the late spring and early summer of 1826. Seized by a severe fever on July 3, Jefferson realized that his death was imminent but was determined to hold on until the following day—the fiftieth anniversary of the adoption of the Declaration of Independence. With his family gathered around, he prepared for the end. Later that night, Jefferson awoke and asked his doctor, "Is it the fourth yet?" They were among his final words.

The following day, Jefferson died in his sleep at 1:10 p.m. Five hours later and nearly six hundred miles away, at 6:20 p.m. at Braintree Farm, Massachusetts, President John Adams also breathed his last. Adams, noting the significance of the date, remarked, "It is a great day. It is a *good* day." Unaware of Jefferson's passing, Adams's final words were "Jefferson still lives." The two men, longtime friends and rivals, passed from life within hours of each other on the 50th birthday of the country to whose service they had dedicated their lives, their fortunes, and their sacred honor. Not only did they see America through her tumultuous infancy, but also nurtured her growth into a respected global presence to carry her into the future.

When it unfolded, the Barbary War was no more than a ripple in the much larger waters of world politics. Bashaw Yusuf had declared war on America by the absurd act of chopping down an American flagstaff. Thomas Jefferson, as president of the first democracy of the modern era, responded in a manner that he, as one of the great political philosophers of his or any time, thought right. Today, the war's military legacy cannot be ignored. It saw the emergence of the U.S. Navy as a force to be reckoned with in foreign seas. It saw the American flag planted for the first time in victory on terrain outside the Western Hemisphere. It saw the first fight in which U.S. Navy gunfire worked in concert with United States land forces. So great was the war's significance for the Marines that their hymn refers to "the shores of Tripoli," and the Corps adopted the Mameluke sword as part of its officers' uniforms in 1825. Most important, here in the twenty-first century, the broader story—the great confrontation between the United States and militant Islamic states—has a new significance.

To Jefferson's way of thinking, the captivity of American seamen and the interference with American commerce demanded a strong military response. The subject was one he had been considering for many years. It had been the subject of many discussions between him and his friend John Adams, back in their ministerial days, in 1780s Europe. In fact, they had set the terms of the debate very clearly.

Adams had told his solemn friend he thought it possible to buy a peace.

Jefferson had countered, "I should prefer the obtaining of it by war."

In response to events on the Barbary Coast, Jefferson, in 1801, had dispatched a small U.S. Navy squadron to the Mediterranean. For the next four years, he responded to circumstances, expanding the fleet to a much larger naval presence. In the end, thanks to the bold leadership of men like Preble and Decatur and Eaton and O'Bannon, military force had helped regain national honor. Even the Federalists, who liked little that Jefferson did, came to accept that the United States needed to play a military role in overseas affairs.

In the end, it was Mr. Jefferson, not Mr. Adams, who won the argument.

EPILOGUE

C aptain Stephen Decatur must have smiled as he sailed the Barbary Coast in 1815. This time he did not sneak in under cover of night, bravely risking his life to destroy a captured American ship. This time he was not leading outnumbered Americans into a battle. And this time he would not leave without getting what he came for.

Perhaps Decatur's smile saddened as he sailed through the waters where his brother had been slain, but the sharpest pangs of grief had dulled in the eleven years since James's death. During the first few years after the Treaty of Tripoli, America had enjoyed the partial peace purchased by the blood of brave men like James Decatur, and now Stephen had the honor of making the peace complete.

William Eaton's instinct that not going for absolute victory was a mistake had been proven correct. During the War of 1812, at the urging of the British, the Barbary pirates had begun taking Americans prisoner again. After the Treaty of Ghent had ended the second war with Great Britain in 1815, the United States Congress authorized an American military presence to return to the Maghreb. The dey of

Algiers had declared war on the United States, and Decatur was commissioned to put an end to the Barbary threat once and for all.

His fleet included his flagship, the USS *Guerriere,* and nine other warships; it was the largest naval force the United States had ever sent to sea. Once in Mediterranean waters, Decatur made short work of dispatching the Algerian leader's navy. He first captured the old enemy ship the *Meshuda.* Two days later, the fleet intercepted the *Estedio* and made it his prize. Both battles were concluded in less than half an hour each. Decatur took nearly five hundred prisoners.

When Decatur reached Algiers harbor on June 28, with the captured sailors and the pride of the Algerian navy under his command, the dey realized that he had made a grave mistake in provoking the Americans into another fight. Backed by his impressive naval force, Decatur obtained a peace treaty within forty-eight hours. This time the treaty called for no payment of tribute. Instead, the terms called for the immediate release of all remaining American hostages (at that point, only ten), $10,000 paid in restitution for merchandise stolen from American ships, full shipping rights guaranteed to all American ships, and no further demands for any future tributes.

Setting out from Algiers, Decatur sailed to Tunis. There he also reached a peace agreement with similar terms and once again insisted that the Barbary state pay reparations. In return for two American ships the Tunisians had captured, they paid Decatur a tribute of $60,000.

Finally, Decatur moved on to Tripoli, the Barbary city where his greatest adventures—and greatest loss—had occurred. Here he demanded that Bashaw Yusuf pay the Americans $30,000 in compensation for Tripolitan interference with American ships during the War of 1812. Decatur insisted upon the release of prisoners from other nations, besides just the United States. He even secured the freedom of British sailors, despite the fact that their nation had so recently been at war with his own. It was a bold, unprecedented move that was celebrated across Europe. America's newfound prestige was not blinded by its own power; might and mercy could work in harmony.

On learning of the outcome of Decatur's mission, the American minister to the Court of St. James's, John Quincy Adams, who now occupied the same post his father had a generation earlier, wrote to Decatur, "I most ardently pray that the example, which you have given, of rescuing our country from the disgrace of a tributary treaty, may become our irrevocable law for all future times."[1] Along the Barbary Coast, the centuries-old practice of building economies around kidnappings, theft, and terror was at last brought to a close. The war that had begun on Jefferson's watch was at last resolved on Madison's.

ACKNOWLEDGMENTS

I know that readers often skip the acknowledgments when they breeze through a book, but I urge you to make an exception here because this project was a true team effort. Unlike our last book, *George Washington's Secret Six*, which was on a subject I had been studying since 1988, this book had a shorter runway, but the passion and intensity of the research were even greater.

First, I have to credit my role models for this project and for *GWSS*, beginning with the most vital: Roger Ailes. I always sectioned off my love of history from my passion for news, but talking with and observing Roger Ailes shape Fox News, it became clear to me that the only way to truly appreciate how special this nation is is to understand our past and the hurdles we had to clear to even exist. There are two other people I have to credit for inspiring me from afar: Bill O'Reilly and Glenn Beck. They were the first news hosts I saw soar to success while always providing a sense of history and relevance. Glenn often did it as an element of his show and Bill has completed a series of American history books that have sold tens of millions of copies. This helped me realize that there is a need for books like this and that so many of our viewers are passionate readers as well!

Now in terms of this project, it's always a thrill working with Don Yaeger, one of this nation's finest authors, and his incredible cohort Tiffany Yecke Brooks. Tiffany has an unmatched work ethic; she is smarter and more humble than anyone I know and was indispensable in this book's completion (and—dare I say?—success). I must mention that Tiffany had the wisdom to marry a Marine, so maybe that explains the passion she had for telling this great story.

Special thanks to Adrian Zackheim, president and publisher of Sentinel, for believing in us to tell the story and for editing and encouraging us over the last three years. Of course, nothing happens without our amazing agent, Bob Barnett. Without the respect Bob has earned in this business we would not have had the good fortune to work with Sentinel on our first project, let alone come back for this one. He works hard, is available almost anytime you need him, and always sports a smile. Thanks, Bob!

If you can keep a secret let me also tell you about one of the stars of the book business, Bria Sandford. She defines the word "indispensable." You rarely get to work with someone who is so deadline oriented but never shows stress or sacrifices creativity. Bria has all those skills. Her ability to help us find our voice in this project and put it on the page was almost magical. Her assistant, Kaushik Viswanath, was also a big help in the process.

As for research, the first person I called when we were considering doing this book was University of Virgina's director of politics, Dr. Larry Sabato. His blessing was vitally important, as was the introduction and meeting with Jim Sofka. Jim might just be the most respected scholar on the Barbary War period and UVA must be thrilled to have him; his kindness and insight were truly needed and appreciated. Hugh Howard was also a huge ally for this book and his encyclopedic knowledge of American history is mind-boggling.

I can't overstate how moving it was to see the great lengths the Marine Corps History Division took to make this book complete. The department is led by Dr. Charles P. Neimeyer, a great leader and just a great all-around person. He's surrounded by an incredible can-do team that includes Ms. Annette D. Amerman (Historian, Marine Corps History Division), Mr. Gregory L. Cina (Archivist, Marine Corps Archives), Ms. Beth L. Crumley (Historian, Marine Corps History Division), and Colonel Peter J. Ferraro, USMC, Retired (Historian, Marine Corps History Division).

It is with great admiration that I would like to thank Congresswoman Marsha Blackburn. She helped clear my path in Washington, opening doors and guiding me through the National Archives/Jefferson Collection.

The best place to research Thomas Jefferson will always be his estate in Monticello and that's where Anna Berkes stepped up big for us. When you research our third president, you are dealing with a man who accomplished enough for ten lifetimes and it can be overwhelming, to say the least. As a research librarian at the Jefferson Library, Anna has knowledge of the president's work that was invaluable, along with her patience! Special thanks, too, for the great tour of the grounds.

Of course, this project wouldn't get off the ground without the support of the Fox News family and no acknowledgments section would be complete without saluting their loyalty. VP Bill Shine has to keep two networks rolling, but still finds time to advise and guide me on my books and I love that he has a special affinity for great

American stories. Suzanne Scott and Shari Berg have been sensational supporters, despite their wide swath of work responsibilities.

Since 1997, I have had the chance to cohost *Fox and Friends*, which is the foundation of my eighteen-year stay at the channel, and knowing the morning show team was behind me was extremely humbling. Despite being in charge of twenty-eight hours of LIVE TV a week and having families of their own, Executive Producers Lauren Petterson and Jennifer Rauchet constantly expressed great enthusiasm for a book and topic they knew little about, but showed boundless curiosity to support. Senior Producers Gavin Hadden, Sean Groman, and Megan Albano have been vital to my completing this project and their skill in weaving the book into our show is noted and appreciated.

I also have to salute my *Fox and Friends* cohosts, Steve Doocy and Elisabeth Hasselback. Their preparation, performance, and patriotism have been inspiring to me through the construction of this story and I look forward to introducing America to this slice of American history with both of these pros by my side. As viewers know, I am always privileged to appear alongside superstar *Friends* anchors Heather Nauert, Ainsley Earhardt, and Heather Childers, and weathercaster Maria Molina. And, of course, the *Fox and Friends* franchise would not be complete without the weekend ratings champs Tucker Carlson, Clayton Morris, and Anna Kooiman.

I look forward to bringing the story to my radio family and fans on *Kilmeade and Friends* as well. First, I have to thank Alyson Mansfield. As senior producer she goes above and beyond on a daily basis, and when the book launches it gets four times as hard—yet she somehow always makes it work. She has heard the play-by-play of this book from concept to completion and her feedback along the way has been invaluable. Harry Kapsalis and Eric Albeen, you have also heard me talk about and work through this book and watched me sign thirty thousand copies. I appreciate all your support and hard work every day.

On the planning and promotion front, Will Weisser and Tara Gilbride at Sentinel showed leadership and enthusiasm that set a great tone for the rollout. Taylor Fleming is a true pro and innovator who seems to never rest when it comes to working on our behalf. Preparation for this promotion began six months ago and George Uribe, founder of Guest Booker, has been endlessly creative and innovative; in fact, I think he likes the book even more than I do (which is a great feeling)! His secret weapons, Molly Polcari and Victoria Delgado, have made it their mission to spread the word on this project and are often the most spirited on our weekly conference calls. As you know, so much of today's sales are done over the Internet and heading up that operation are Paul Guest and Lindsay Wallace, two talented and vital cogs in the wheel of success. I cannot thank them enough.

Last and most important, thanks to the world's best family. My wife, Dawn, and children Bryan, Kirstyn, and Kaitlyn—this is why I have been working late and spending hours reading, writing, and reviewing instead of playing or spending more time with you. Thanks for understanding or at least pretending to. I hope when you read this you will decide that it was worth it!

In conclusion, this book (like *George Washington's Secret Six*) features historic figures of huge importance playing supporting roles to relatively unknown, unsung patriots. This book is dedicated to all those who fight our wars and never seek or receive the credit they deserve. It's up to the next generation to tell their stories, because without the Americans fighting in the trenches and on the seas, we would not be able to enjoy life as citizens of the world's greatest economic and military superpower.

NOTES

PROLOGUE: UNPREPARED AND UNPROTECTED

1. Richard O'Brien to Thomas Jefferson, August 24, 1785.

CHAPTER 1: AMERICANS ABROAD

1. Elizabeth Wayles Eppes to Thomas Jefferson, October 13, 1784.
2. Thomas Jefferson to Mary Jefferson, September 20, 1785.
3. Mary Jefferson to Thomas Jefferson, ca. May 1786.
4. Thomas Jefferson to Francis Eppes, August 30, 1785.
5. Ibid.
6. Thomas Jefferson to Francis Eppes, December 11, 1785.
7. Lambert, *The Barbary Wars*, p. 16.
8. Thomas Jefferson to Nathaniel Greene, January 12, 1785.
9. M. Le Veillard to Dr. Franklin, October 9, 1785.
10. John Adams to Thomas Jefferson, February 17, 1786.
11. Ibid.
12. John Adams to John Jay, February 20, 1786.
13. Thomas Jefferson to William Carmichael, May 5, 1786.
14. George Washington address to Congress, December 30, 1790.

15. "American Commissioners to John Jay," March 28, 1786.
16. John Adams to Thomas Jefferson, July 3, 1786.
17. Thomas Jefferson to John Adams, July 11, 1786.
18. John Adams to Thomas Jefferson, July 31, 1786.

CHAPTER 2: SECRETARY JEFFERSON

1. Thomas Jefferson to James Monroe, November 11, 1784.
2. "Mediterranean Trade," December 30, 1790.
3. Ibid.
4. David Humphreys to Michael Murphy, October 6, 1793.
5. Edward Church to Thomas Jefferson, October 12, 1793.
6. "Appointment of Joel Barlow as U.S. Agent, Algiers," February 10, 1796.
7. Eaton, *The Life of the Late Gen. William Eaton*, p. 17.
8. Ibid., pp. 19–20.
9. Ibid., p. 26.

CHAPTER 3: THE HUMILIATION OF THE USS *GEORGE WASHINGTON*

1. Log of the USS *George Washington*.
2. Ibid.
3. Richard O'Brien to the secretary of state, May 16, 1800.
4. London, *Victory in Tripoli* (2005), p. 4.
5. Richard O'Brien to the secretary of state, September 20, 1800.
6. Ibid.
7. William Bainbridge to Richard O'Brien, October 9, 1800.
8. Richard O'Brien to William Eaton, October 19, 1800.
9. Log of the USS *George Washington*.
10. William Eaton, personal note on letter to Richard O'Brien, October 19, 1800.

CHAPTER 4: JEFFERSON TAKES CHARGE

1. "Treaty of Peace and Friendship Between the United States of America and the Bey and Subjects of Tripoli of Barbary."
2. William Eaton to Timothy Pickering, June 24, 1800.
3. Dearborn, *The Life of William Bainbridge*, p. 40.
4. Jefferson, notes, May 15, 1801–April 8, 1803.
5. Ibid.

CHAPTER 5: A FLAGPOLE FALLS

1. Joel Barlow to the secretary of state, August 18, 1797.
2. James L. Cathcart, "Circular Letter," February 21, 1801.
3. James L. Cathcart to Secretary of State James Madison, May 11, 1801.
4. Ibid., May 16, 1801.
5. James L. Cathcart to Nicholas C. Nissen, May 15, 1801.
6. James L. Cathcart to Secretary of State James Madison, June 4, 1801.

CHAPTER 6: THE FIRST FLOTILLA

1. Richard Dale to Andrew Sterett, July 30, 1801.
2. Captain Richard Dale to the secretary of the navy, July 2, 1801.
3. Ibid.
4. Captain Richard Dale to Samuel Barron, July 4, 1801.

CHAPTER 7: SKIRMISH AT SEA

1. Richard Dale to the dey of Algiers and the bey of Tunis, July 10, 1801.
2. William Eaton to James Madison, July 10, 1801.
3. Eaton, *The Life of the Late Gen. William Eaton,* p. 59.
4. William Eaton, "Journal," February 22, 1799.
5. William Eaton to Secretary of State Timothy Pickering, June 15, 1799.
6. William Eaton to Eliza Eaton, April 6, 1799.

7. William Eaton to Secretary of State Timothy Pickering, June 15, 1799.

8. Richard Dale to the secretary of the navy, July 19, 1801.

9. Richard Dale to the bashaw of Tripoli, July 25, 1801.

10. Richard Dale to Andrew Sterett, July 30, 1801.

11. Extract of a letter from Andrew Sterett.

12. "Capture of the Ship of War *Tripoli* by U.S. Schooner *Enterprize*," *National Intelligencer and Washington Advertiser*, November 18, 1801.

13. Newton Keene to William W. Burrows, August 10, 1801.

14. "Capture of the Ship of War *Tripoli* by U.S. Schooner *Enterprize*," *National Intelligencer and Washington Advertiser*, November 18, 1801.

15. Thomas Jefferson, "Presidential Message," December 8, 1801.

CHAPTER 8: PATIENCE WEARS THIN

1. Annals of Congress, Seventh Congress, First Session, pp. 325–26.

2. Newton Keene to William W. Burrows, September 28, 1801.

3. James Brown to James Leander Cathcart, September 16, 1801.

4. Richard Dale to the secretary of the navy, December 13, 1801.

5. Ibid.

6. Richard Dale to William Bainbridge, December 15, 1801.

7. William Eaton to Secretary of State James Madison, September 5, 1801.

8. Edwards, *Barbary General*, p. 95.

9. William Eaton to James Madison, September 5, 1801.

10. Richard O'Brien to James Madison, July 22, 1801.

CHAPTER 9: THE DOLDRUMS OF SUMMER

1. Henry Wadsworth, from his personal journal, September 13, 1802, reprinted in *Naval Documents*.

2. Richard V. Morris to the secretary of the navy, May 31, 1802.

3. Alexander Murray to the secretary of the navy, June 1, 1802.

4. William Eaton to James Madison, August 9, 1802.

5. Secretary of the navy to Richard V. Morris, April 20, 1802.

6. William Eaton to James L. Cathcart, April 26, 1802.

7. Alexander Murray, "Journal of the U.S. Frigate *Constellation*," July 22, 1802.

8. Cooper, *History of the Navy of the United States of America* (1856), pp. 157–58.

9. Alexander Murray, "Journal of the U.S. Frigate *Constellation*," July 22, 1802.

10. Alexander Murray to the secretary of the navy, July 30, 1802.

11. William Eaton to James Madison, August 23, 1802.

12. Secretary of the navy to Richard V. Morris, April 20, 1802.

13. Richard V. Morris to the secretary of the navy, October 15, 1802.

14. Thomas Jefferson to Albert Gallatin, March 28, 1803.

15. William Eaton to Hamet Qaramanli, August 6, 1802.

16. James L. Cathcart, journal notes for James Madison, March 14, 1803.

17. Richard V. Morris to the secretary of the navy, March 30, 1803.

18. Abbot, *The Naval History of the United States*, p. 189.

19. "Journal of Midshipman Henry Wadsworth," April 2, 1803.

20. Eaton, *The Life of the Late Gen. William Eaton*, p. 244.

21. Secretary of the navy to Richard V. Morris, June 21, 1803.

22. "Concerning Commodore Morris' Squadron in the Mediterranean."

23. Thomas Jefferson to Phillip Mazzei, July 18, 1804.

24. William Eaton to James Madison, August 23, 1802.

CHAPTER 10: THE OMENS OF OCTOBER

1. Edward Preble to Mary Deering, August 13, 1803.

2. Quoted in Flexner, *George Washington and the New Nation*, vol. 3, pp. 321–22, 377.

3. Secretary of the navy to Edward Preble, August 2, 1803.

4. Ibid., July 13, 1803.

5. Edward Preble to the secretary of the navy, September 23, 1803.

6. Edward Preble, *Diary*, October 6, 1803.

7. Edward Preble, quoted in Tucker, *Dawn Like Thunder*, p. 205.

8. Tobias Lear to Mrs. Lear, October 13, 1803.

9. Ralph Izard Jr. to Mrs. Ralph Izard Sr., October 11, 1803.

10. Edward Preble to the secretary of the navy, October 10, 1803.

11. Emperor of Morocco to Thomas Jefferson, October 11, 1803.

12. Edward Preble to Mary Deering, ca. October 1803.

CHAPTER 11: THE *PHILADELPHIA* DISASTER

1. William Bainbridge to Edward Preble, November 12, 1803.

2. William Bainbridge to Tobias Lear, February 8, 1804.

3. William Bainbridge to Susan Bainbridge, November 1, 1803.

4. Whipple, *To the Shores of Tripoli*, p. 118.

5. Cowdery, in Baepler, *White Slaves, African Masters*, p. 162.

6. Ibid., p. 190.

7. Ibid., p. 191.

8. Shaw, *A Short Sketch*, p. 23, reprinted in Baepler, *White Slaves, African Masters* (1999), p. 19.

9. William Bainbridge to the Secretary of the Navy, November 1, 1803.

CHAPTER 12: BY THE COVER OF DARKNESS

1. Edward Preble to Mary Deering, November 20, 1803.

2. Charles Stewart to Susan Decatur, December 12, 1826.

3. Edward Preble to the secretary of the navy, December 10, 1803.

4. Tucker, *Stephen Decatur*, pp. 42–43.

5. Dearborn, *The Life of William Bainbridge*, p. 60.

6. William Bainbridge to Edward Preble, December 5, 1803.

7. Edward Preble to the secretary of the navy, January 17, 1804.

8. Edward Preble to Stephen Decatur, January 31, 1804.

9. Ibid.

10. Morris, *The Autobiography of Commodore Charles Morris, U.S. Navy* (Boston: A. Williams, 1880), p. 27.

11. Lewis Heermann, quoted in McKee, *Edward Preble: A Naval Biography, 1761–1807* (1972), p. 197.

12. Ralph Izard Jr. to Mrs. Ralph Izard Sr., February 20, 1804.

13. William Ray, *Horrors of Slavery; or, The American Tars in Tripoli* (2008), p. 76.

14. Ibid.

CHAPTER 13: THE BATTLE OF TRIPOLI

1. Stephen Decatur to Keith Spence, January 9, 1805.

2. Edward Preble to the secretary of the navy, February 3, 1804.

3. *New York Evening Post,* March 28, 1804.

4. Secretary of the navy to Edward Preble, May 22, 1804.

5. James Madison to Thomas FitzSimons, April 13, 1804.

6. The oft-quoted words might or might not have been Nelson's but have long been attributed to him, though by a biographer some forty years after the burning of the USS *Philadelphia*. Allen, *Our Navy and the Barbary Corsairs* (1905), p. 173.

7. George Davis to the secretary of state, March 26, 1804.

8. Edward Preble to the secretary of the navy, June 14, 1804.

9. Edward Preble to Richard O'Brien, June 13, 1804.

10. Preble, *Diary,* June 14, 1804.

11. Eaton, *The Life of the Late Gen. William Eaton,* p. 242.

12. Ibid., p. 262.

13. Edwards, *Barbary General* (1968), p. 131.

14. Eaton, *The Life of the Late Gen. William Eaton,* p. 265.

15. Thomas Jefferson to John Page, June 25, 1804.

16. James Madison to Tobias Lear, June 6, 1804.

17. Secretary of the navy to Samuel Barron, June 6, 1804.

18. Edward Preble to James L. Cathcart, May 28, 1804.

19. Edward Preble to the secretary of the navy, September 18, 1804.

20. Ibid.; McKee, *Edward Preble: A Naval Biography, 1761–1807,* p. 262.

21. Stephen Decatur to Keith Spence, January 9, 1805.

22. Edward Preble to the secretary of the navy, September 18, 1804.

23. Mackenzie, *Life of Stephen Decatur,* p. 97.

24. Edward Preble to the secretary of the navy, September 18, 1804.

25. Dearborn, *The Life of William Bainbridge, Esq.*, pp. 74–75.

26. Edward Preble to Mary Deering, quoted in McKee, *Edward Preble: A Naval Biography, 1761–1807* (1972), p. 307.

CHAPTER 14: OPENING A NEW FRONT

1. William Eaton to Congressman Samuel Lyman, October 12, 1801.

2. William Eaton to Alexander Ball, December 13, 1804.

3. William Eaton, "Journal," December 7, 1804.

4. William Eaton to the secretary of the navy, December 13, 1804.

5. Hamet Qaramanli to William Eaton, January 3, 1805.

6. Alexander Murray to Richard V. Morris, August 22, 1802.

CHAPTER 15: WIN IN THE DESERT OR DIE IN THE DESERT

1. William Eaton, "Journal," April 2, 1805; *The Life of the Late Gen. William Eaton*, p. 317.

2. William Eaton, *The Life of the Late Gen. William Eaton*, p. 323.

3. William Eaton, "Journal," April 2, 1805; *The Life of the Late Gen. William Eaton*, p. 323.

4. Eaton, ibid., April 16, 1805; ibid., p. 329.

5. Eaton,ibid.," April 25, 1805; ibid., p. 330.

6. William Eaton to the Governor of Derne, April 26, 1805; ibid., p. 337.

7. William Eaton to Samuel Barron, April 29, 1805; ibid., p. 337.

8. Ibid.

9. Edwards, *Barbary General* (1968), p. 214.

CHAPTER 16: ENDGAME

1. Tobias Lear to John Rodgers, May 1, 1805.

2. Jonathan Cowdery, "Journal," May 24, 1805.

3. William Eaton, "Journal," May 12, 1805; *The Life of the Late Gen. William Eaton*, p. 340.

4. William Eaton to Samuel Barron, May 29, 1805.

5. William Eaton to John Rodgers, June 13, 1805.

6. Timothy Pickering to unknown, March 21, 1806.

7. "Report of the Committee," March 17, 1806.

CHAPTER 17: FAIR WINDS AND FOLLOWING SEAS

1. *National Intelligencer,* November 6, 1805.

EPILOGUE

1. John Quincy Adams to Stephen Decatur, quoted in Mackenzie, *Decatur*, p. 27.

A NOTE ON SOURCES

A book like this could not exist if not for the documents—the letters, the journals, the ships' logs, and the rest—left by the participants. A compilation of the most essential of those is to be found in *Naval Documents Related to the United States Wars with the Barbary Powers* (1939–1944). The encyclopedic contents of this six-volume set must form the basis of any book written on this subject.

Another essential primary source is the collection called *American State Papers*. In effect, it is Congress's diary, and contains reports, letters, and other materials, as well as congressional motions and minutes. It is available online at http://memory.loc.gov/ammem/amlaw/lwsp.html.

As the page-by-page source notes suggest, the personal papers of the participants have also been invaluable: the collected papers of Thomas Jefferson, John Adams, and George Washington have all been published in richly annotated editions that are generally available. Less accessible are the papers of Tobias Lear (not published but in the archives of the Clements Library at the University of Michigan) and Edward Preble (Library of Congress). Numerous other players in this drama left memoirs and correspondence. Many of those documents have been published and are listed in the bibliography below, including writings from James Leander Cathcart, many of the Barbary captives (among them William Ray and Elijah Shaw), and, in particular, the remarkable William Eaton.

Numerous other writers have written on this subject over the last two centuries, and below you'll find a selected list of the best of the primary and secondary works.

Abbot, Willis J. *The Naval History of the United States.* New York: Dodd, Mead and Company, 1896.

Adams, Henry. *History of the United States During the Administration of Thomas Jefferson.* New York: Library of America, 1986.

Allen, Gardner W. *Our Navy and the Barbary Corsairs.* Boston: Houghton Mifflin Company, 1905.

Allison, Robert J. *The Crescent Obscured.* New York: Oxford University Press, 1995.

Baepler, Paul. *White Slaves, African Masters: An Anthology of American Barbary Captivity Narratives.* Chicago: University of Chicago Press, 1999.

Cathcart, James Leander. *Tripoli: First War with the United States.* La Porte, IN: Herald Print, 1901.

Cogliano, Francis D. *Emperor of Liberty: Thomas Jefferson's Foreign Policy.* New Haven, CT: Yale University Press, 2014.

Cooper, J. Fenimore. *History of the Navy of the United States of America.* New York: Stringer and Townsend, 1856.

Cunningham, Noble E., Jr. *The Process of Government Under Jefferson.* Princeton, NJ: Princeton University Press, 1978.

Dearborn, H. A. S. *The Life of William Bainbridge, Esq., of the United States Navy.* Princeton, NJ: Princeton University Press, 1931.

Eaton, William. *The Life of the Late Gen. William Eaton.* Brookfield, MA: E. Merriam & Co., 1813.

Edwards, Samuel. *Barbary General: The Life of William H. Eaton.* Englewood Cliffs, NJ: Prentice-Hall, Inc., 1968.

Ellis, Joseph J. *American Sphinx: The Character of Thomas Jefferson.* New York: Alfred A. Knopf, 1996.

Ferguson, Eugene S. *Truxtun of the Constellation: The Life of Commodore Thomas Truxtun, U.S. Navy, 1755–1822.* Baltimore, MD: Johns Hopkins University Press, 1959.

Flexner, James Thomas. *George Washington.* 4 vols. Boston: Little, Brown & Co., 1965–1972.

Irwin, Ray D. *Diplomatic Relations of the United States with the Barbary Powers: 1776 1816.* Chapel Hill: University of North Carolina Press, 1931.

Kimball, Marie. *Jefferson: The Scene of Europe.* New York: Coward-McCann, Inc., 1950.

Kitzen, Michael L. S. *Tripoli and the United States at War: A History of American Relations with the Barbary States, 1785–1805.* Jefferson, NC: McFarland & Co., Inc., 1992.

Lambert, Frank. *The Barbary Wars.* New York: Hill and Wang, 2005.

Lane-Poole, Stanley. *The Story of the Barbary Corsairs.* New York: G. P. Putnam's Sons, 1890.

London, Joshua E. *Victory in Tripoli: How America's War with the Barbary Pirates Established the U.S. Navy and Built a Nation.* New York: John Wiley & Sons, Inc., 2005.

McCullough, David. *John Adams.* New York: Simon & Schuster, 2001.

McKee, Christopher. *Edward Preble: A Naval Biography, 1761–1807.* Annapolis, MD: Naval Institute Press, 1972.

Mackenzie, Alexander Slidell. *Life of Stephen Decatur, Commodore in the U.S. Navy.* Boston: Charles C. Little and James Brown, 1846.

Magoun, F. Alexander. *The Frigate Constitution and Other Historic Ships.* New York: Dover Publications, 1987.

Malone, Dumas. *Jefferson and His Time.* 6 vols. Boston: Little, Brown & Company, 1948–1981.

Morris, Charles. *The Autobiography of Commodore Charles Morris, U.S. Navy.* Boston: A. Williams, 1880.

Nash, Howard P. Jr. *The Forgotten Wars: The Role of the U.S. Navy in the Quasi War with France and the Barbary Wars, 1798–1805*. South Brunswick, NJ: A. S. Barnes & Co., 1968.

Naval Documents Related to the United States Wars with the Barbary Powers. 6 vols. Washington, DC: Government Printing Office, 1939–1944.

Parker, Richard B. *Uncle Sam in Barbary: A Diplomatic History*. Gainesville: University Press of Florida, 2004.

Quincy, Josiah. *Figures of the Past from the Leaves of Old Journals*. Boston: Roberts Brothers, 1883.

Ray, William. *Horrors of Slavery; or, The American Tars in Tripoli*. New Brunswick, NJ: Rutgers University Press, 2008.

Shaw, Elijah. *A Short Sketch of the Life of Elijah Shaw*. Rochester, NY: Strong & Dawson, 1843.

Sumner, Charles. *White Slavery in the Barbary States*. Boston: P. J. Jewett and Company, 1853.

Toll, Ian W. *Six Frigates: The Epic History of the Founding of the U.S. Navy*. New York: W. W. Norton and Company, 2006.

Tucker, Glenn. *Dawn Like Thunder: The Barbary Wars and the Birth of the U.S. Navy*. Indianapolis: Bobbs-Merrill Company, 1963.

Tucker, Spencer. *Stephen Decatur: A Life Most Bold and Daring*. Annapolis, MD: Naval Institute Press, 2005.

Whipple, A. B. C. *To the Shores of Tripoli: The Birth of the U.S. Navy and Marines*. William Morrow and Company, Inc., 1991.

Wright, Louis B., and Julia H. Macleod. *The First Americans in North Africa: William Eaton's Struggle for a Vigorous Policy Against the Barbary Pirates, 1799–1805*. Princeton, NJ: Princeton University Press, 1945.

Zacks, Richard. *The Pirate Coast: Thomas Jefferson, the First Marines, and the Secret Mission of 1805*. New York: Hyperion, 2005.

INDEX

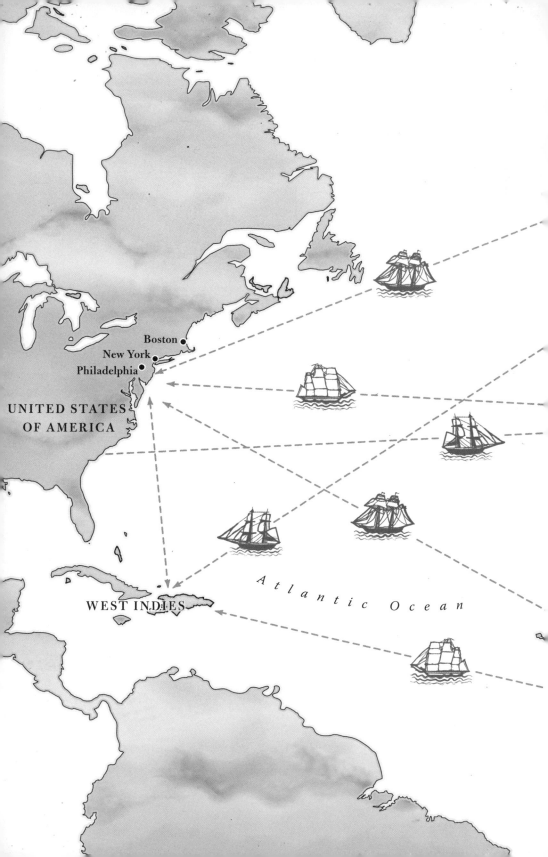